P-47
THUNDERBOLT

in detail & scale

Bert Kinzey

squadron/signal publications

COPYRIGHT © 1998 BY DETAIL & SCALE, INC.

This book is a product of Detail & Scale, Inc., which has sole responsibility for its content and layout, except that all contributors are responsible for the security clearance and copyright release of all materials submitted. Published by Squadron/Signal Publications, 1115 Crowley Drive, Carrollton, Texas 75011.

CONTRIBUTORS AND SOURCES:

Jeff Ethell
Warren Bodie
Lloyd Jones
David Menard
Dana Bell
Bill Paul
Norris Graser
Clark Macomber

Paul Gold
J. C. Bahr
Jim Roeder
Stan Parker
Frank Mitchell
Jeff Zimmerman
Kieth Liles
Steve Dyckes

Bill Klears
U. S. Air Force Museum
Museum of Aviation, Warner Robins, Georgia
U. S. Air Force Armament Museum
Yanks Air Museum, Chino, California
Planes of Fame Museum, Chino, California
Vintage Fighters, Jeffersonville, Indiana

Detail & Scale, Inc. and the author express a special "thank you" to Bob Spaulding and his volunteers at the U. S. Air Force Museum for their help during the preparation of this publication. Appreciation is also expressed to the Research Division of the Air Force Museum whose assistance was essential. Stan Hoefler of the Yanks Air Museum in Chino, California, is also deserving of special recognition. Finally, Bill Paul of the Museum of Aviation at Warner Robins, Georgia, is worthy of very special recognition for his time, patience, and support. Detail & Scale, Inc. highly recommends these excellent museums to all aviation enthusiasts.

Many photographs in this publication are credited to their contributors. Photographs with no credit indicated were taken by the author.

DEDICATION:
TO JEFF ETHELL
Thanks for all your help through the years.
We miss you.

Jeff Ethell personally took the photographs on page 48 specifically for this publication. For years, Jeff assisted the author with the Detail & Scale Series, providing valuable color photographs and other assistance. Most valued was his respect and personal support. In June 1997, Jeff was killed while flying a P-38 Lightning. He is sorely missed.

ISBN 1-888974-07-9

Above (front cover photo): A P-47D-20-RE named "Belle of Belmont" taxis out for a mission over Europe. This Thunderbolt was assigned to the 56th Fighter Group.
(Mark Brown/USAFA via Bodie)

Right (rear cover photo): Details on the instrument panel in a P-47D-30-RA are illustrated in this large photograph. For additional photographs of this Thunderbolt's cockpit, see pages 40 and 41.

INTRODUCTION

When viewed from the front, the Thunderbolt's large R-2800 radial engine and the eight .50-caliber machine guns illustrate the power of the aircraft's design. While many people might argue about the P-47's eye appeal when compared to more streamlined designs like the P-51 Mustang, no one could deny its power and rugged dependability. It was these features, not its appearance, that made it successful in combat. **(USAFM)**

"If you wanted to have your picture taken so you could send it home to your girl, you sat in the cockpit of a P-51 Mustang. If you wanted to survive in combat, you climbed into the cockpit of a P-47 Thunderbolt."

"If you were in combat and you wanted to come home, you'd better pray you were in a Thunderbolt."

Hubert "Hub" Zemke repeated these often-quoted statements to the author as he signed a numbered, limited-edition lithograph of a P-47D created by aviation artist Jerry Crandall. Zemke, who commanded the famed 56th Fighter Group during World War II, was always very resolute in his support of the Thunderbolt, but his sentiments were echoed by thousands of fighter pilots who flew Republic's big "Jug" in every theater of World War II. Both statements reflect the rugged dependability of the P-47 that brought many a pilot safely back home after sustaining battle damage that would have destroyed almost any other fighter.

But the Thunderbolt was not only more survivable, it could dish it out as well. It was the most heavily armed single-engine fighter in World War II. It had twice the firepower of most Mustangs, and fifty percent more than the P-51D Mustang, P-40 Warhawk, F6F Hellcat, or F4U Corsair. Its guns could quickly dispatch an enemy fighter or destroy many targets on the ground. While the Mustang was sleek and certainly had considerable eye appeal, there were also those who believed that the large rugged appearance of the Thunderbolt better exemplified what a fighter should look like.

Much has been written about the Thunderbolt, and its developmental and operational histories could and have

filled many volumes. It is the purpose of this publication to only briefly summarize the development of the aircraft while focusing attention on the physical details of each of the production variants.

Hundreds of USAAF photographs were examined to find those that best illustrate the design and features of the aircraft. No less than ten existing Thunderbolts were photographed extensively to show every detail from the propeller hub to the position light on the rudder. Among these aircraft is the P-47D-30-RE on display at the Museum of Aviation in Warner Robins, Georgia. That aircraft was taken right off the flight line and retained for exhibit in 1947. It remains today with its original equipment, and all paint in the cockpit, wheel wells, and other interior surfaces are the original paint applied at the factory. It is the only Thunderbolt that is now on display without any subsequent restoration in these areas.

Jeff Ethell, Jim Roeder, Norris Graser, and the author also photographed other P-47s, often removing panels, opening cockpits, and repositioning control surfaces and the intercooler doors in order to provide the most detailed and accurate look at this famous fighter ever published. Most of the detailed photographs on the following pages were taken specifically for this publication. Additionally, Lloyd Jones created all new scale drawings which correct a number of errors found in previously published drawings of the P-47.

Our usual Modelers Section can be found at the back of the book, and Thunderbolt kits from the 1950s to the present are reviewed. All presently available models from 1/144th scale through 1/32nd scale are included.

This is also the first book in the Detail & Scale Series to be expanded to eighty pages in length. The color section has been doubled in size so that almost twice the amount of color photographs can be included. Color art is also being added for the first time to illustrate the development of paint schemes and markings used on the aircraft. This larger format with the additional color pages will remain a standard feature on all future titles in the Detail & Scale Series.

DEVELOPMENTAL HISTORY

The Republic XP-44 Rocket was never built, because its intended engine, the Pratt & Whitney R-2180 radial, was unsuccessful. However, the lines of its design are unmistakenly those that ultimately became the P-47 Thunderbolt. *(USAFM)*

Alexander De Seversky was born in Southern Russia in 1894. After attending the Russian Naval Academy, he became a pilot. During World War I, he was credited with downing thirteen German aircraft, but he lost a leg in combat. While in the United States in 1917 to study U. S. aircraft programs, Seversky defected because of concerns about the Russian Revolution in his homeland. He quickly became involved with the newly established U. S. Army Air Corps, both as a test pilot and a design engineer. Throughout the 1920s, he remained involved with the development of aviation within the U. S. military.

In 1931 he started the Seversky Aircraft Corporation at Farmingdale, New York. He joined forces with Alexander Kartveli, a fellow Russian who had already established an excellent reputation as an aeronautical engineer. This two-man team began to design, develop, and test their own aircraft beginning with the SEV-3 amphibian. After modifying it to a land plane design and making several improvements to increase performance, the Seversky Aircraft Corporation received its first contract to build thirty of these aircraft for the U. S. Army. They became the BE-8, which was the first low-wing monoplane trainer to enter Air Corps service.

Seversky's second design was similar to the first, but it had semi-retractable landing gear and only one seat. Development of this design culminated in the P-35 fighter which was ordered by the USAAC in 1936. It was powered by the Pratt & Whitney R-1830 radial engine which offered 850 horsepower.

Continuing advancements in powerplant design, specifically the development of a supercharger, led Seversky to propose a more powerful development of the P-35. Designated the XP-41 by the Army, the new design retained the P&W R-1830 radial engine of the P-35, but it was fitted with a geared supercharger that boosted horsepower to 1150. This extra power, along with a sleeker design that included a fully retractable landing gear, provided a considerable improvement over the performance of the P-35. The last production P-35 was converted to the sole XP-41 prototype, but no orders for production aircraft were placed. It would become the last Seversky-built aircraft delivered to the USAAC.

During this same time period, there were problems of a business nature at the Seversky Aircraft Corporation. Although that is a different story, it did lead to a number of changes, the most noticeable of these being that the company was renamed the Republic Aircraft Corporation on September 15, 1939. Alexander Kartveli remained as vice-president and chief design engineer.

The exhaust driven turbosupercharger offered the next increase in performance, but where to locate it within the airframe of a fighter was the question. Kartveli decided on mounting it in the lower aft fuselage, a location which had never been tried before. This approach proved successful, and the two-stage turbosupercharger boosted the horsepower of the R-1830-35 engine to 1,200 for take off. The design became known as the YP-43 Lancer, and the first of thirteen prototypes was deliv-

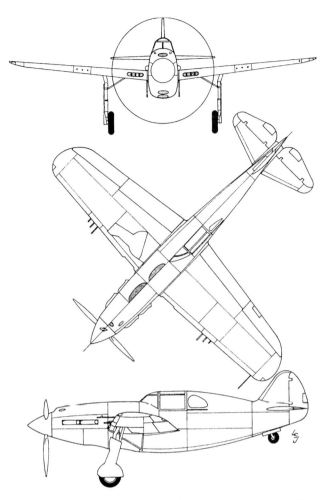

The small XP-47A was never built, and it was considerably different in appearance from the XP-47B that followed. It featured an inline liquid cooled engine.
(Drawing by Lloyd S. Jones)

ered for testing in September 1940. By now, the lines that would eventually become the P-47 Thunderbolt were becoming readily identifiable. Fifty-four P-43s and 205 P-43As and A-1s were built, but in October 1942, they were redesignated RP-43s (restricted) and prohibited from use in combat. Some were provided to China, while those retained by the U. S. Army were fitted with cameras and used as photo-reconnaissance aircraft.

Pratt & Whitney was developing the R-2180 radial, and Kartveli planned it for use in a further development of the YP-43 design which became known as the XP-44 Rocket. Although an order for eighty P-44s was placed, problems with the R-2180 caused its cancellation, and no XP-44s were built. These aircraft were subsequently completed as P-43 Lancers.

Although the R-2180 was a failure, Pratt & Whitney's larger R-2800 proved to be an outstanding success. Capable of producing 2000 horsepower, it became the most powerful production radial engine in the world at that time. Kartveli modified the P-44 design to accept the new engine and the designation was changed to P-44-2. The Army initially ordered 225 P-44-2s, but this was increased to 827 in September 1940.

Meanwhile, Republic was also working on a design which had been designated XP-47 by the Army. It was

radically different from any of the radial engined aircraft Seversky/Republic had produced, and it was to be powered by an inline, liquid-cooled, Allison V-1710 engine. It was sleek, small, and lightweight, everything that the P-44 was not. XP-47 and XP-47A prototypes were ordered in November 1939 and January 1940 respectively, but before work could be started on either, the Army issued a new set of specifications for its next generation fighter. While others were opting for the sleek inline engines, Kartveli revived his design with the big 2000 horsepower Pratt & Whitney radial. His design would be the heaviest single-engine fighter in the world, and it was also the most heavily armed with eight .50-caliber machine guns.

In August 1940, the Army modified the existing XP-47 contract by issuing Change Order #2. This cancelled the XP-47 and XP-47A designs, and replaced them with the XP-47B. With this change, the P-47 instantly went from being a small lightweight fighter with a liquid-cooled inline engine to a heavyweight brute with a large frontal cross section housing a huge radial engine.

The XP-47B made its initial flight on May 6, 1941, less than ten months after Change Order #2 had been issued. This short period of time was undoubtedly due to the similarities the design shared with the previous P-43 and XP-44. But initial testing revealed some problems that had to be fixed, most importantly that the fabric control surfaces had to be replaced with those covered with a metal skin. The left side entry door was soon deleted in favor of a sliding framed canopy.

The urgency caused by the war in Europe meant that an order for 773 production P-47Bs was placed before all of the bugs could be worked out. These aircraft began rolling off the assembly lines before all of the problems were known, much less fixed. They were delivered with fabric-covered control surfaces, and this was to cause numerous failures and crashes.

The first unit to receive the P-47B was the 56th Fighter Group which was based on Long Island, not far from the Republic Plant. Accidents plagued their use of the P-47B until the fabric control surfaces were replaced with those having a metal skin. The tremendous speed of the aircraft, particularly when diving, required some getting used to, and both pilot and airframe had to go through the learning process. After all, the P-47 was twice as heavy as many contemporary single-engine

The first of the Thunderbolts was the single XP-47B prototype. While many refinements would be made to the design over the next five years, the basic lines of the original Thunderbolt remained essentially unchanged.
(USAFM)

The P-47B could be identified by the radio mast on the spine which was angled forward. While a few were assigned to the 56th Fighter Group, P-47Bs were not considered suitable for combat. In 1944, they were redesignated RP-47Bs with the "R" standing for "Restricted."
(USAFM)

P-47C-2-RE, 41-6245, was assigned to the 495th FTG when this nice in-flight photo was taken. Note that the cowl flaps only come down to the centerline of the fuselage, and there is no bulged keel added to this aircraft. However, bulged keel kits were retrofitted to a number of P-47Cs. The C-models were the first to feature the eight-inch fuselage extension associated with the Quick Engine Change package. P-47Cs were delivered with the standard Olive Drab over Neutral Gray camouflage scheme, so it is unusual to see one in a natural metal finish. The use of a large national insignia under both wings was common in the European Theater of Operations. (USAFM)

fighters, and it was a handful for any pilot.

At first, the huge Thunderbolt was the brunt of jokes and less-than-complimentary nicknames. Because the shape of its fuselage resembled a milk jug, it was often called the "Jug," but by the end of World War II, this nickname was applied with far more affection than it was at first.

Required changes were incorporated on the assembly lines, and the number of P-47Bs built was reduced to only 170. None of these saw combat, and in 1944, they were redesignated RP-47s to indicate a restricted status.

P-47Cs were produced with metal-covered control surfaces, and they had a strengthened tail section. They could be identified from the previous P-47B due to the fact that their antenna masts (when fitted) were mounted vertically rather than being slanted forward. A total of 57 P-47Cs and 55 P-47C-1-REs were built, but like the earlier P-47Bs, these were not considered ready for combat. It was aircraft from the P-47C-2-RE and P-47C-5-RE production blocks that became the first Thunderbolts sent to the European Theater of Operations (ETO). On April 8, 1943, P-47Cs of the 4th Fighter Group flew their first missions

and got their baptism of fire. The 4th FG was soon joined by the 78th and then the 56th Fighter Groups as the first Thunderbolt units.

As these fighter squadrons earned their spurs, the diving speed of the huge fighter proved to be a considerable advantage in disengaging from an unfavorable situation with an enemy aircraft. The firepower from the eight machine guns was another major benefit of the design. Ground crews found that maintenance and serviceability were excellent. But there were also disadvantages, and the most severe of these was the limited range. The big

All production models of the Thunderbolt were fitted with eight wing-mounted .50-caliber machine guns, more than in any other American single-engine fighter of World War II. In the photo above, shell casings and links are expended from slots beneath the wings as the guns are test fired. At right, armorers load the ammunition into the gun bays and clean the barrels. (Both USAFM)

The first version of the Thunderbolt to be produced in large quantities was the P-47D. All versions from the P-47D-1-RE to the P-47D-23-RE were razorbacks with the high spine and framed canopy. This P-47D-23-RE was assigned to the 1st Air Commando Squadron at Asansol, India. The direction-finding loop antenna was sometimes added to the spine of aircraft operating in the China-Burma-India theater where additional navigation equipment was often necessary. *(USAFM)*

This P-47D has yellow and black checks on its vertical and horizontal tails, and it was assigned to the 319th Fighter Squadron of the 325th Fighter Group. This unit was part of the 15th Air Force in Italy. Named "Big Stud," this Thunderbolt was the personal aircraft of Lt. Col. Robert L. Baseler, who was the commander of the 325th FG. A P-47-40-RA named "Big Stud" was flown by Baseler after the war and is shown on page 22. Like this aircraft, it had 88 as its fuselage number. *(USAFM)*

Thunderbolt had been designed as an interceptor, and it proved to be as range-limited as the much smaller Spitfire. Complicating this problem was the fact that the airframe had not been designed to accommodate external fuel tanks.

An interim solution was the use of a rather bulbous centerline tank that looked something like the radar pod that appeared under TBM Avengers after the war. This tank had a capacity of 205 gallons, but it was only practical as a ferry tank. As a result, the keel of the aircraft was redesigned to contain the necessary plumbing for external fuel tanks of various sizes. Since this modification would not be added to the assembly line until well into the production of P-47D, kits were sent to the field to be retrofitted to existing aircraft.

There were likewise no provisions in the original design for carrying stores under the wings. The need for such capability was recognized and would later be incorporated during the production of the P-47D-15-RE, but some existing aircraft had their wings strengthened so that external tanks or bombs could be fitted.

It was the P-47D that became the most numerous of all production variants with 12,602 being delivered. This version was divided into no less than thirty-three production blocks built at both Farmingdale, New York, and Evansville, Indiana. To differentiate between the two,

Thunderbolts built at Farmingdale were designated with an RE suffix, while those coming off the line at Evansville were given an RA suffix.

Throughout the production of the P-47D, numerous improvements and changes were made, but none was more obvious to the eye than the elimination of the razorback spine in favor of a bubble canopy. While this greatly enhanced the pilot's visibility all around the aircraft, it significantly altered the original jug-like appearance of the aircraft. The change to the bubble canopy was made beginning with the P-47D-25-RE and the P-47D-26-RA.

By the end of 1943, P-47Ds had replaced the C-models in combat units, and thousands were being delivered to every theater.

The geography of the Pacific theater was even more of a problem for the short-ranged Thunderbolt, but as the capability for carrying external fuel was improved, more P-47Ds found their way to the combat zones there and in the China-Burma-India theater. It became the first aircraft to deliver napalm in combat during action at Saipan.

As the war in Europe continued, P-47s were used more and more as fighter-bombers. This was not only because of evolving tactics, but also due to the ruggedness of the Thunderbolt's design. Aircraft attacking ground targets take a great deal of fire from the front, and a single hit from even the smallest anti-aircraft gun could

Starting with the P-47D-25-RE, Thunderbolts were fitted with a bubble canopy as seen on this P-47D-28-RE. This greatly improved all-around visibility, but it decreased the lateral stability of the aircraft. This problem was later reduced by the addition of dorsal fins along the top of the spine of the aircraft. *(USAFM)*

Above: Thunderbolts also served with the air forces of several other nations. This P-47D carries the markings of the Forca Aerea Brasileira (Brazil Air Force), and it was attached to the 350th Fighter Group in Italy during 1944. (USAFM)

Right: This P-47D is painted in gray and green camouflage and displays British roundels on the wings and fuselage. Razorback P-47Ds were called Thunderbolt Is by the British, while the bubbletops were designated Thunderbolt IIs. (USAFM)

pierce the coolant tank of an aircraft with a liquid-cooled engine. Once the coolant ran out, the engine would seize, and the aircraft would crash or make a forced landing. But the big radial-engined Thunderbolt proved far more survivable in this dangerous environment, and they were soon carrying rocket tubes and bombs into combat. Combined with eight .50-caliber machine guns, these external stores proved lethal to most ground targets. After the invasion of France, and throughout the push into Germany, P-47Ds also provided close air support to troops on the ground. Many an allied infantryman owed his life to the pilots in the Thunderbolts above.

Back home, Curtiss also opened an assembly line that produced Thunderbolts which were designated P-47Gs. But the five small production blocks of these aircraft were plagued by exceedingly poor quality control and a lack of combat equipment. None had provisions for wing pylons, and some did not have gun sights or other equipment. As

This Free French P-47D has come to some grief after landing in the snow. A total of 446 P-47Ds from several production blocks were provided to the French in Italy and France. Many of these aircraft continued to serve in L'Armée de l'Air after the war was over. (USAFM)

The P-47M, with its R-2800-14W/-57 engine, G. E. CH-5 turbosupercharger, and water injection was used operationally only with the 56th Fighter Group during the closing months of the war. Most were painted in unusual and unofficial camouflage schemes after being received by that unit. This particular P-47M has just arrived in England and has yet to receive a coat of camouflage paint or any unit markings. Also note that the dorsal fin has not yet been added. These were installed after the aircraft arrived in Europe. *(USAFM)*

The long range P-47N had a larger wing with blunt tips. During World War II, this version was used only in the Pacific, where it operated from the island of Ie Shima. Although not originally fitted, rocket launch stubs were later added under the wings of P-47Ns. *(USAFM)*

a result, these were used only in training or hack roles.

The next combat-worthy variant of the Thunderbolt was the P-47M, and only one production block of 130 aircraft was completed as P-47M-1-REs. Equipped with the R-2800 14W 57 "C-series" engine, these were designed to be high speed Thunderbolts which could reach 475 miles-per-hour in level flight. The only unit to fly this version in combat was the 56th Fighter Group in England.

The final production variant of the Thunderbolt was designed specifically to meet the long range requirements in the Pacific, where it was used exclusively during World War II. The P-47N featured a larger redesigned wing, and it was capable of flying missions up to nine hours in duration. This is remarkable testimony to the versatility of a design that had been originally intended to be a short range interceptor. Four fighter groups flew P-47Ns from the island of Ie Shima during the closing months of the war.

At war's end, the Thunderbolt had compiled an enviable record. No less than 545,575 missions had been flown totalling over 1,352,810 hours of flying time. More than 7,000 enemy aircraft had been destroyed by P-47s including 3,752 confirmed aerial victories. Countless thousands of tons of enemy equipment and supplies had been destroyed on the ground along with tanks, trucks,

trains, gun emplacements, buildings, bridges, and every other conceivable type of target. It is commonly thought that the P-47 had largely been replaced by the time the war ended, but the fact is that more than 6,000 were still in service when the Japanese surrendered.

After the war, many Thunderbolts were scrapped, but some were retained and were still in service when the U. S. Army Air Forces became the U. S. Air Force in 1947. Those still in the inventory of the Air Force and the Air National Guard were redesignated F-47s.

During the Korean War, F-51D Mustangs were pressed into service as fighter-bombers and ground support aircraft. Their vulnerability to ground fire resulted in very high loss rates. Many of the pilots who flew these Mustangs in Korea had flown Thunderbolts during World War II, and they openly expressed their desire to have their rugged survivable warriors in service again.

Thunderbolts last saw combat in the Dominican Republic in 1964. The last ones in service were retired in Peru during 1969. When production ended in December 1945, 15,683 Thunderbolts had been built. This was the highest number of any U. S. fighter in history. Considering the high unit cost of fighters today and the different methods of waging war, one can say with certainty that this is a record that will always belong to the P-47.

When the U. S. Army Air Forces became the U. S. Air Force in 1947, the Thunderbolts that remained in service with both the regular Air Force and the Air National Guard were redesignated F-47s. This F-47D-40-RA is painted in regular Air Force markings and shown shortly after the change in designation. *(USAFM)*

P-47 VARIANTS

XP-47B

Only one XP-47B was built, and it was originally natural metal with "U. S. ARMY" stencilled in black under the wings. It was later painted in the Olive Drab over Neutral Gray camouflage as used on the production P-47Bs. This aircraft was destroyed in a crash on August 8, 1942.   (USAFM)

With the cancellation of the lightweight XP-47A in August 1940, one XP-47B (RE), 40-3051, was ordered, and this was the prototype of the Thunderbolt series. It was very similar in design to the XP-44 Rocket, and it made its first flight from Republic's Farmingdale plant on May 6, 1941. Exhaust fumes in the cockpit forced pilot Lowry Brabham to terminate the flight early at nearby Mitchell Field. The problem was traced to some hot oil on the supercharger ducting in the lower fuselage, and it was easily corrected. Otherwise, the flight confirmed the promise of the design.

The XP-47B continued in the flight test program and reached 412 miles-per-hour in level flight. On August 8, 1942, it was destroyed in a crash after the rear fuselage caught fire during a test flight, but by this time, production P-47Bs had joined the flight evaluation program.

Distinctive features of the prototype included a hinged door, which provided access to the cockpit from the left side, and a small stub antenna mast that was located just aft of the cockpit on the spine. Rear glass panels, shorter, but similar to those on a P-40, were fitted to the sides of the spine to provide limited visibility to the rear. The Pratt & Whitney R-2800-17 engine was installed with a Curtiss Electric constant-speed propeller which was 12' 2" in diameter. As delivered, the prototype was natural metal and devoid of any markings except for "U. S. ARMY" being lettered in black under the wings. By the time it was lost, it had been painted in the Olive Drab over Neutral Gray camouflage, and it had the blue disc and white star type national insignia on the fuselage and wings.

Model XP-47B
Number built 1

ENGINE . . . . P&W R-2800-17

PERFORMANCE
  Max Speed . . . . 412 mph
  Cruising Speed . . . . 280 mph
  Max Range/Altitude . . . . 1,150 miles/10,000 feet
  Normal Range/Altitude . . . 575 miles/25,000 feet
  Service Ceiling . . . . 38,000 feet
  Climb . . . . 5 minutes to 15,000 feet

WEIGHTS
  Empty . . . . 9,189 pounds
  Gross Take off . . . . 12,500 pounds

DIMENSIONS
  Span . . . . 40 feet, 9.25 inches
  Wing Area . . . . 300 square feet
  Length* . . . . 35 feet, 4 inches
  Height . . . . 14 feet, 2 inches

FUEL
  Internal . . . . 305 gallons
  External . . . . None

* Length varied slightly with change in rudder design.

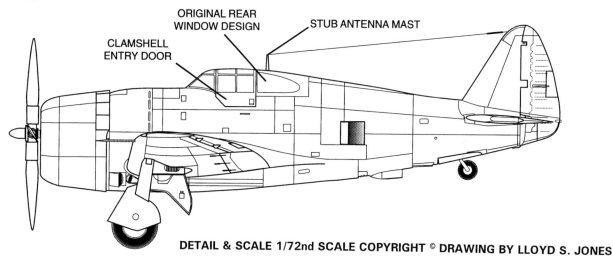

CLAMSHELL ENTRY DOOR
ORIGINAL REAR WINDOW DESIGN
STUB ANTENNA MAST

DETAIL & SCALE 1/72nd SCALE COPYRIGHT © DRAWING BY LLOYD S. JONES

P-47B

This early production P-47B has a turtledeck window on each side of the fuselage, but these were not on many aircraft. The first two and last P-47Bs had the stub antenna mast and clamshell door as used on the XP-47B. All other production P-47Bs had the longer antenna mast that angled forward and the sliding framed canopy that was standard on all razorback Thunderbolts.   (USAFM)

The first two P-47Bs were essentially copies of the XP-47B, including the stub antenna mast and the clamshell door on the left side of the cockpit. The last P-47B built was also initially completed to this configuration, and it later became the XP-47E. This aircraft was modified to have a pressurized cockpit, and this added 400 pounds of weight to the airframe. Although originally fitted with an R-2800-21 engine, it later had an R-2800-59 engine, a Hamilton-Standard propeller, and full cowl flaps installed.

The third production P-47B was the first to have the sliding framed canopy, but the windscreen on this aircraft

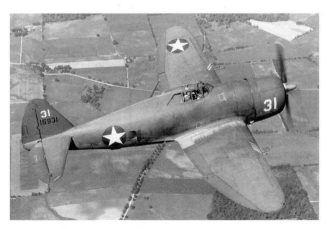

A flying view of a later RP-47B (RE) shows the elimination of the turtledeck windows. P-47Bs initially had fabric-covered control surfaces, but metal covered rudders and elevators were retrofitted to most examples of this variant.   (USAFM)

was unique in that it had a flat front panel. A turtledeck window was installed on each side of the spine, but this feature was not on many production aircraft. A longer antenna mast, which was angled forward, was also first introduced on this aircraft. This longer mast was associated with the installation of SCR-283 radio equipment, and the reason it was angled forward was to provide clearance for the sliding framed canopy. All other Thunderbolts in the single P-47B (RE) production batch of 170 aircraft had the angled windscreen that was standard on all subsequent razorback Thunderbolts, the sliding framed canopy, and the angled antenna mast.

The first five P-47Bs, 41-5895 through 41-5899, were considered pre-production aircraft, and they joined the prototype in the flight test program. Two were destroyed in crashes, one of which killed test pilot George Burrell. In June 1942, the 56th Fighter Group started to receive the P-47B as the first operational unit with Thunderbolts. They would remain the only unit ever equipped with P-47Bs, and these aircraft would never see combat.

Additional problems surfaced at Mitchell Field where the 56th was training, and a series of accidents plagued their transition to the big new fighter. The two crashes, as well as some of the problems experienced by the 56th FG, were attributed to the fabric-covered control surfaces and empennage failure. As a result, a change was made to metal-skinned surfaces, the rudder was redesigned, and the rear fuselage section was strengthened. Aircraft already off the production line were retrofitted with these improvements. Until they could be made, limitations were placed on flight maneuvers and diving speeds.

There were minor problems as well. Ignition failures at high altitudes had to be corrected by pressurizing the ignition system, and problems with oil circulation in the turbosupercharger had to be solved. Equally important was that the pilots of the 56th Fighter Group had to learn to fly an aircraft that was much bigger and heavier than anything they had known before. Some became amazed at the tremendous speeds they could attain in dives, but they had no previous experience with the problems that compressibility caused when it came to controlling the

P-47B COCKPIT DETAILS

The photograph above shows the general layout of the cockpit in a P-47B, while the other three photos on this page illustrate and identify the features on the instrument panel and both sides of the cockpit. Note the corrugated floor used in early Thunderbolts. *(All USAFM)*

P-47B Instrument Panel

1. Landing Gear, Tail Wheel, & Flap Position Indicator	13. Ignition Switch
2. Florescent Light	14. Fuel Quantity Gage
3. Fuel Level Warning Light	15. Kollsman Altimeter
4. Turn Indicator	16. Hydraulic Pressure Gage
5. Air-Speed Indicator	17. Compass
6. Bank and Turn Indicator	18. Parking Brake
7. Artificial Horizon	19. Clock
8. Fuel Pressure Warning Light	20. Rate of Climb Indicator
9. Suction Gage	21. Tachometer
10. Vacuum Gage Selector Valve	22. Manifold Pressure Gage
11. Carburetor Air Temp. Gage	23. Fuel Pressure Gage
12. Propeller Anti-Icer Control	24. Oil Temp. & Pressure Gage
	25. Cylinder Head Temp. Gage

P-47B, Cockpit, Left Side

1. Spotlight	10. Propeller Anti-Icer Control
2. Trim Tab Control Group	11. Ignition Switch
3. Flap Control Lever	12. Gun Heat Control Lever
4. Shutter Position Indicators	13. Safety Latch
5. Gun Safety Switch	14. Landing Gear Control Lever
6. Propeller Safety Light	15. Fuel Selector Valve
7. Throttle Quadrant	16. Main Switch Box
8. Panel Light	17. Circuit Breakers
9. Landing Gear Warning Horn Switch	

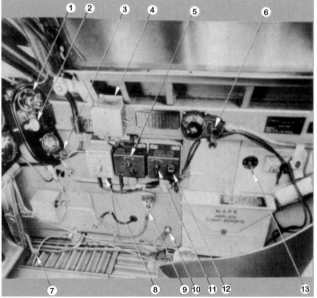

P-47B, Cockpit, Right side

1. Engine Primer	8. Radio Switch Box
2. Cowl Flap Control	9. Cockpit Vent Control
3. Oxygen Regulator	10. Tail Wheel Lock
4. Identification Keying Switches	11. Radio Receiver Volume Control Selector Switch
5. Transmitter Emission Control Switch	12. Radio Receiver and Transmitter Filament "On-Off" Control Knob
6. Radio Tuning Dial Control	13. "Hi-Lo" Switch
7. Rudder Pedal Adjustment Lever	

P-47Bs had cowl flaps that extended down to approximately the centerline of the fuselage. None of them had the eight-inch fuselage extension or the bulged keel which were introduced on later versions. This particular aircraft was one of a few P-47Bs modified to carry cameras and serve in the reconnaissance role. These aircraft were initially called RP-47Bs, but this designation was later used for all P-47Bs to denote a restricted flying status. *(USAFM)*

The last production P-47B was fitted with the clamshell cockpit entry door like that found on the XP-47B and the first two production P-47Bs. Notice that the original rear window design was also used. This aircraft served as the test bed for a fighter with a pressurized cockpit, and it was redesignated the XP-47E. The Hamilton-Standard propeller was also evaluated on this Thunderbolt, and it was fitted by the time this photograph was taken in the snow at Wright Field. *(USAFM)*

plane and recovering from the dive. As a result, there were a number of accidents that ended as large holes in the ground. But gradually the pilots not only came to understand the unique flying characteristics of the big bird, they were able to use its capabilities to considerable advantage.

A few P-47Bs were configured as photographic reconnaissance aircraft and redesignated RP-47Bs. This program was short lived, but the RP-47B designation would later reappear in 1944 with a different meaning. Because of the lessons learned from the flight test program and the 56th Fighter Group's early experience, it was evident that the P-47Bs were not worthy of combat. They were relegated to training and other secondary roles, and the RP-47B designation was reapplied meaning "restricted."

Model P-47B
Number built 170

ENGINE . . . . P&W R-2800-21

PERFORMANCE
Max Speed/Altitude . . . . . . 429 mph/27,800 feet
Cruising Speed . . . . 335 mph
Max Range/Altitude . . . . . 835 miles/10,000 feet
Normal Range/Altitude . . . 550 miles/25,000 feet
Service Ceiling . . . . 42,000 feet
Climb . . . . 6.7 minutes to 15,000 feet

WEIGHTS
Empty . . . . 9,346 pounds
Gross . . . . 12,245 pounds
Max Take off . . . . 13,360 pounds

DIMENSIONS
Span . . . . 40 feet, 9.25 inches
Wing Area . . . . 300 square feet
Length . . . . 35 feet, 4 inches
Height . . . . 14 feet, 2 inches

FUEL
Internal . . . . 305 gallons
External . . . . None

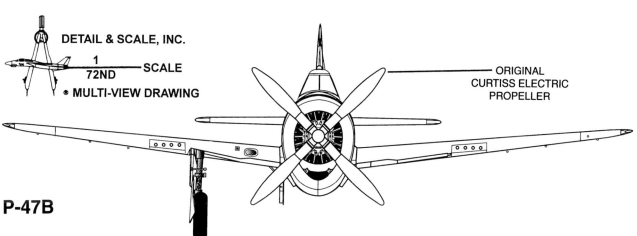

DETAIL & SCALE, INC.
$\frac{1}{72ND}$ SCALE
® MULTI-VIEW DRAWING

ORIGINAL
CURTISS ELECTRIC
PROPELLER

P-47B

DETAIL & SCALE 1/72nd SCALE COPYRIGHT © DRAWINGS BY LLOYD S. JONES

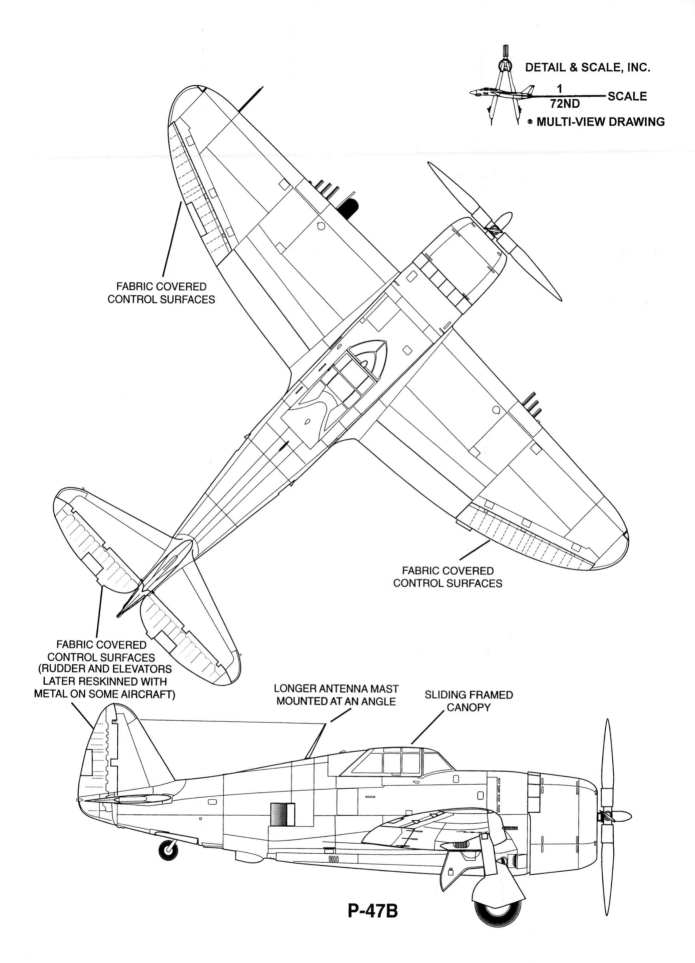

DETAIL & SCALE, INC.

$\dfrac{1}{72\text{ND}}$ ——— SCALE

® MULTI-VIEW DRAWING

FABRIC COVERED
CONTROL SURFACES

FABRIC COVERED
CONTROL SURFACES

FABRIC COVERED
CONTROL SURFACES
(RUDDER AND ELEVATORS
LATER RESKINNED WITH
METAL ON SOME AIRCRAFT)

LONGER ANTENNA MAST
MOUNTED AT AN ANGLE

SLIDING FRAMED
CANOPY

P-47B

DETAIL & SCALE 1/72nd SCALE COPYRIGHT © DRAWINGS BY LLOYD S. JONES

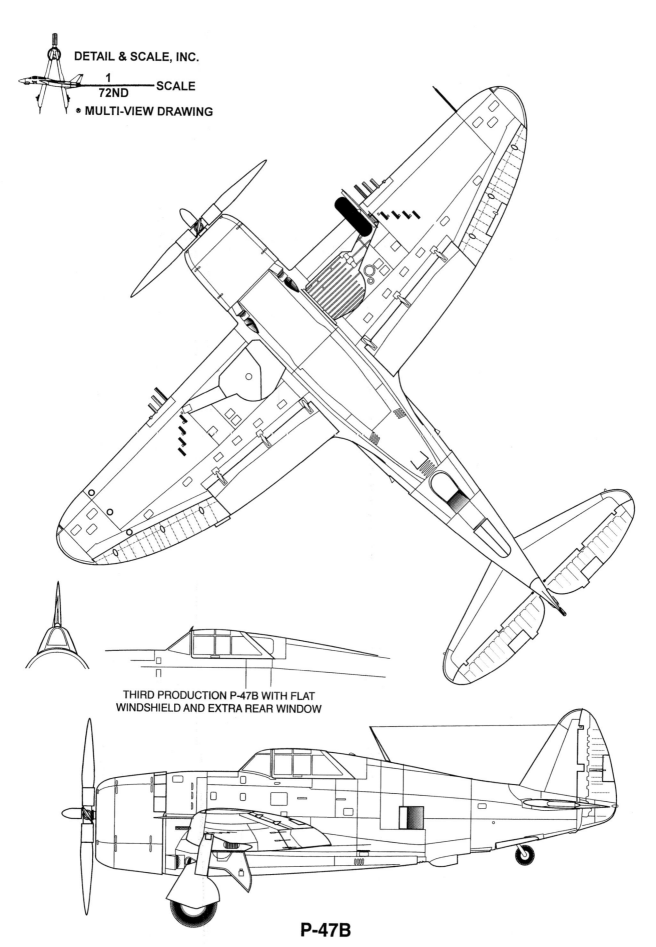

DETAIL & SCALE, INC.

$\dfrac{1}{72\text{ND}}$ ——— SCALE

® MULTI-VIEW DRAWING

THIRD PRODUCTION P-47B WITH FLAT
WINDSHIELD AND EXTRA REAR WINDOW

P-47B

DETAIL & SCALE 1/72nd SCALE COPYRIGHT © DRAWINGS BY LLOYD S. JONES

P-47C

The P-47C-RE was the first production block of P-47Cs. They were essentially similar to P-47Bs, except that they had metal-covered control surfaces to include the ailerons. The radio mast was mounted vertically on the spine, so it became an easy way to visually distinguish a P-47C from the previous variant. **(USAFM)**

The second production variant of the Thunderbolt was divided into four production blocks totaling 602 aircraft. The first of these was simply called the P-47C-RE and these fifty-seven aircraft were in most ways similar to the previous P-47B. A change in radios to the SCR-515-A meant that the mast on the spine could be mounted vertically, and this visual identifier was the easiest way to distinguish an early P-47C from the P-47B. Not visible to the eye was the improved oxygen system, A-17 turbosupercharger regulator, and a new gun camera.

More important to the pilot were the metal covered control surfaces to include the ailerons as well as the elevators and rudder. The tail units were strengthened after several failures had been experienced in the test program. But for essentially the same reasons as the P-47B, the Thunderbolts in this first block of P-47Cs were also withheld from combat.

Aircraft in the second production block were desig-

nated as P-47C-1-REs, and these were the first to be produced with an eight-inch extension in the forward fuselage which was associated with a Quick Engine Change (QEC) package. As a bonus, this eight-inch extension also improved the handling characteristics of the aircraft. Another less noticeable new feature of this production block was the addition of a deflector plate between the oil cooler door and the exhaust waste gate on each side of the lower forward fuselage. Minor improvements were made to the landing gear, and the tail wheel steering was eliminated. The ducting and shroud for the turbosupercharger was revised, and a hydraulic flap equalizer was added. But because of the fact that the fifty-five P-47C-1-REs had no capability to carry extra fuel externally, none were ever used in combat operations.

The P-47C-2-RE had provisions to carry external fuel in a bulbous 205-gallon tank beneath the fuselage. But this unpressurized tank proved far from adequate and was not satisfactory for anything other than ferry flights. Nevertheless, a few of the 128 P-47C-2-REs produced were assigned to the 4th, 78th, and 56th Fighter Groups, and these were the first Thunderbolt units to enter combat in that order.

Early combat experience immediately revealed problems with the radio gear, and this led to a changeover to

After sustaining battle damage to its tail section, this P-47C-2-RE brought its pilot safely home. The MX fuselage codes indicate that this Thunderbolt was assigned to the 82nd Fighter Squadron of the 78th Fighter Group. This was the second P-47 unit to see combat. **(USAFM)**

This P-47-C-5-RE has only a whip antenna on the spine which is barely visible in the photograph. Although the P-47C is usually associated with the European Theater of Operations, this Thunderbolt was assigned to the 58th Fighter Group in New Guinea. **(USAFM)**

British equipment. P-47C-2-REs and P-47C-5-REs were often seen without the usual radio mast on the spine.

The final 362 examples of this variant were designated P-47C-5-REs, and they had only equipment and detail changes when compared to the earlier P-47C-2-RE. Many of these were subsequently retrofitted with what became known as a "bulged keel" kit which altered the outline of the lower fuselage. This kit, which was added in the field, included the plumbing and shackle that permitted the use of a dropable belly tank that was suitable for combat operations. Alternately, a 500-pound bomb could also be carried. The bulged keel, with its shackle and plumbing, would later become a production standard beginning with the P-47D-5-RE.

P-47Cs were produced with cowl flaps that came down only to the horizontal centerline of the aircraft. But some were retrofitted with two additional lower flaps on each side, and this feature became standard early in the production of P-47Ds.

Model P-47C
Number built 602

Data below for: P-47C-1-RE

ENGINE . . . . P&W R-2800-21

PERFORMANCE

Max Speed/Altitude . . . . . . 433 mph/30,000 feet
Cruising Speed . . . . 350 mph
Max Range/Altitude . . . . . 835 miles/10,000 feet
Normal Range/Altitude . . . 400 miles/25,000 feet
Service Ceiling . . . . 42,000 feet
Climb . . . . 11 minutes to 20,000 feet

WEIGHTS

Empty . . . . 9,900 pounds
Gross . . . . 13,500 pounds
Max Take off . . . . 14,925 pounds

DIMENSIONS

Span . . . . 40 feet, 9.25 inches
Wing Area . . . . 300 square feet
Length . . . . 36 feet, 1 inch
Height . . . . 14 feet, 3.3 inches

FUEL

Internal . . . . 305 gallons
External* . . . . 205 gallons

* 205 gallons in an unpressurized ferry tank on the P-47C-2-RE and the P-47C-5-RE only. Some aircraft in these blocks retrofitted to carry dropable tanks of a smaller size in combat.

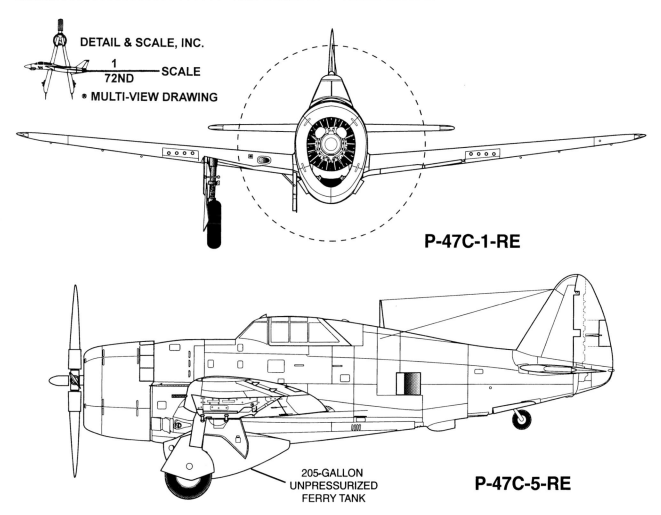

DETAIL & SCALE, INC.

$\frac{1}{72ND}$ SCALE • MULTI-VIEW DRAWING

P-47C-1-RE

205-GALLON UNPRESSURIZED FERRY TANK

P-47C-5-RE

DETAIL & SCALE 1/72nd SCALE COPYRIGHT © DRAWINGS BY LLOYD S. JONES

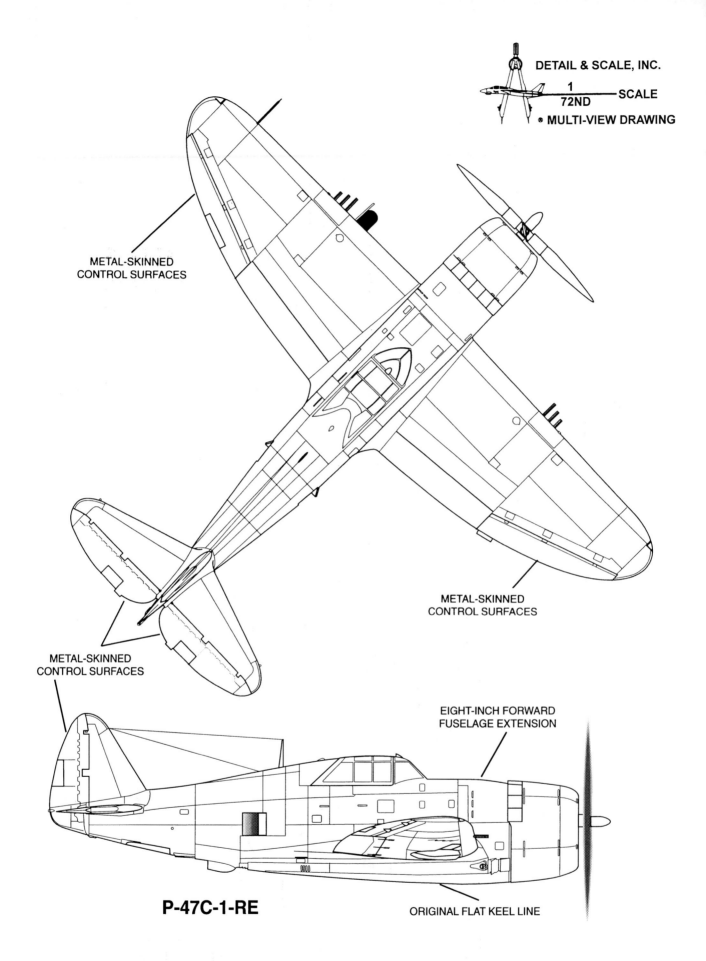

METAL-SKINNED
CONTROL SURFACES

METAL-SKINNED
CONTROL SURFACES

METAL-SKINNED
CONTROL SURFACES

EIGHT-INCH FORWARD
FUSELAGE EXTENSION

P-47C-1-RE

ORIGINAL FLAT KEEL LINE

DETAIL & SCALE 1/72nd SCALE COPYRIGHT © DRAWINGS BY LLOYD S. JONES

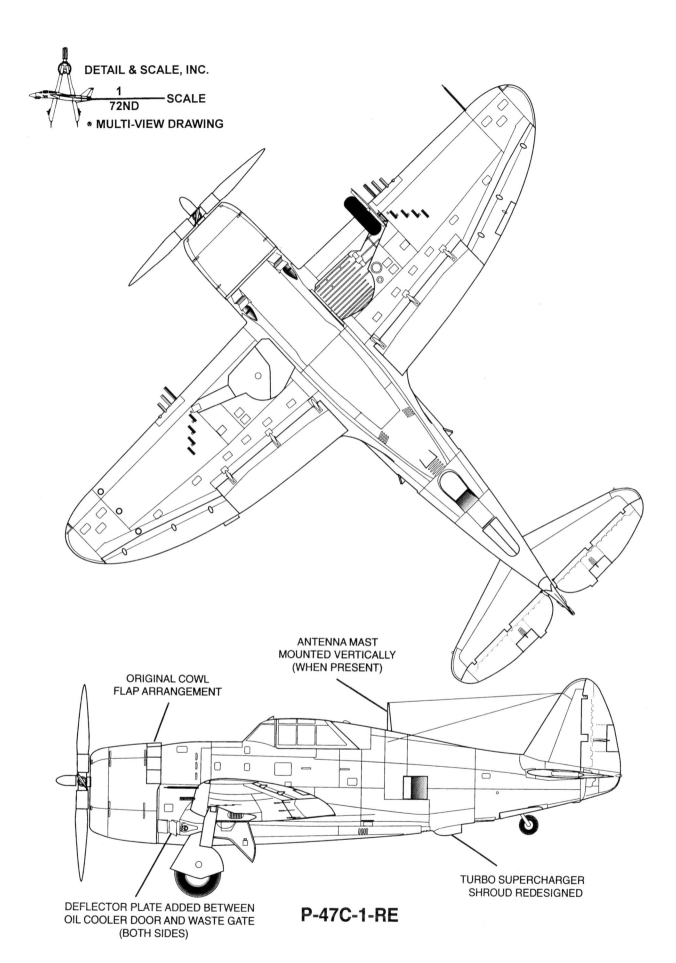

ANTENNA MAST
MOUNTED VERTICALLY
(WHEN PRESENT)

ORIGINAL COWL
FLAP ARRANGEMENT

DEFLECTOR PLATE ADDED BETWEEN
OIL COOLER DOOR AND WASTE GATE
(BOTH SIDES)

P-47C-1-RE

TURBO SUPERCHARGER
SHROUD REDESIGNED

DETAIL & SCALE 1/72nd SCALE COPYRIGHT © DRAWINGS BY LLOYD S. JONES

P-47C COCKPIT DETAILS

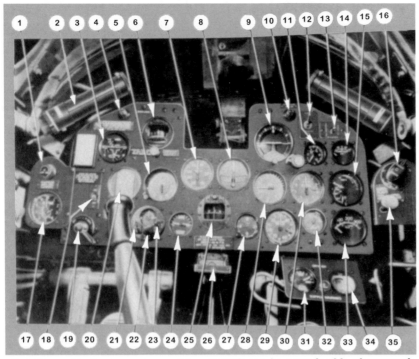

1. Propeller Anti-Icer Control
2. Florescent Light
3. Landing Gear Tail Wheel & Flap Position Indicator
4. Fuel Level
5. Altimeter
6. Turn Indicator
7. Air Speed Indicator
8. Bank and Turn Indicator
9. Artificial Horizon
10. Fuel Pressure Warning Lamp
11. Suction Gage
12. Vacuum Gage Selector Valve
13. Starter Switch
14. Carburetor Air Temp. Gage
15. Oil Temp. & Pressure Gage
16. Engine Primer
17. Turbo Tachometer
18. Master Battery Switch
19. Ignition Switch
20. Fuel Quantity Gage
21. Contactor Switch
22. Contactor (Pip Squeak)
23. Contactor Clock Switch
24. Hydraulic Pressure Gage
25. Compass
26. Parking Brake Handle
27. Clock
28. Rate of Climb Indicator
29. Manifold Pressure Gage
30. Tachometer
31. Oxygen Cylinder Pressure Gage
32. Fuel Pressure Gage
33. Cylinder Head Temp. Gage
34. Oxygen Flow Indicator
35. Cowl Flap Control

Details on the instrument panel in a P-47C can be seen in this photograph. Keys for the items indicated are given at right. **(USAFM)**

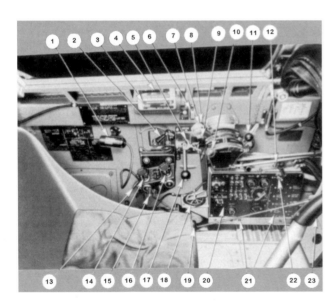

The left side of the cockpit is shown here. Keys are provided below. **(USAFM)**

Items on the right side of the P-47C's cockpit are illustrated in this photo with keys listed below.

1. Cockpit Spotlight
2. Wing Flap Control Handle
3. Intercooler Shutter Indicator
4. Oil Cooler Shutter Indicator
5. Landing Gear Control Safety Lock
6. Gun Safety Switch
7. Throttle
8. Supercharger Control
9. Microphone Push-to-talk Button
10. Mixture Control
11. Propeller Control
12. Landing Gear Warning Horn Switch
13. Propeller Anti-Icing Control
14. Rudder Trim Tab Control
15. Elevator Trim Tab Control
16. Aileron Trim Tab Control
17. Landing Gear Control Handle
18. Fuel Selector Valve
19. Hydraulic Hand Pump
20. Main Switch Box
21. Circuit Breakers
22. Belly Tank Control Switch
23. Control Stick Grip

1. Oxygen Regulator
2. Crystal Filter Selector Switch
3. Command Receiver Control Box
4. Command Transmitter Control Box
5. Identification Lights Switches
6. Contactor Heater Switch
7. IFF Radio Destroyer Buttons
8. Rudder Pedal Adjustment Lever
9. Cockpit Vent Control
10. Tail Wheel Lock
11. Belly Tank Release
12. Pilot's Seat

P-47D

The bulged keel was not fitted at the factory to any P-47Ds until the production of the P-47D-5-RE. However, kits were retrofitted to earlier aircraft as evidenced on this P-47D-2-RE. This particular Thunderbolt was assigned to the 351st Fighter Squadron of the 353rd Fighter Group. Note the lack of an antenna mast on the spine of this aircraft. *(USAFM)*

With a total of 12,602 produced, the P-47D was by far the most numerous Thunderbolt variant. The P-47C, P-47G, and P-47N were the other three versions with more than one production block, and for each of these there were relatively minor changes from one block to another. But with the P-47D, it was an entirely different and curious story. Counting the RP-47D, there were thirty-three production blocks, and often significant changes, both internal and external, were made between two subsequent blocks. The last P-47D-40-RA was almost a completely different airplane than the first Ds that had rolled down the assembly line in early 1942. The fact that the D suffix was not changed in spite of significant modifications and improvements implemented during this entire production run of 12,602 aircraft can be likened to today's F-16C Fighting Falcon. In both cases, knowing the production block to which a given aircraft belongs is essential to understanding its features and capabilities.

Originally, only Thunderbolts built at Evansville were to be designated P-47Ds, much in the same way as the P-51B and P-51C designations had differentiated between identical Mustangs built in California and Texas respectively. But this was subsequently changed, and numerous D-models were produced at both plants. Although the first P-47Ds built at Evansville carried the same RE manufacturer's suffix as had been used by Farmingdale, the system was changed as P-47D production was getting underway. RE continued to be used by the Farmingdale plant, while RA became the manufacturer's suffix for Evansville.

The first four Thunderbolts to carry the D suffix (42-22250 through 22253) were also the first built at Evansville, although the fuselages had been built in New York. They were not much different from the P-47C-5-RE and were subsequently given the restricted RP-47D designation. The next 110 REs (42-22254 through 42-22363) were built at Evansville before the change in manufacturer's suffix, and they too were little different from P-47Cs. They had the original flat keel and cowl flaps that came down only to the aircraft's centerline on each side. Most were assigned to training units in the United States.

The additional cowl flaps became a production standard during the P-47D-1-RE block, while the bulged keel, with its provisions for carrying an external drop tank or bomb, was added to the assembly line with the P-47D-5-RE. The P-47D-4-RA was the first to have provisions for water injection to boost power, but this feature was retrofitted to earlier Ds and Cs. Although some early Ds had their wings strengthened so that external tanks could be carried, stronger wings and pylons did not become a standard feature until production of the P-47D-15-RE.

The P-47D-20-RA had improved heating in the cockpit, and the gun bays were heated through a ducted system instead of by an electrical unit. But the next real change came with the P-47D-22-RE which was the first to have the Hamilton-Standard paddleblade propeller installed at the factory. This was the first of three propellers that had blades with a wider chord which offered increased performance over the original Curtiss Electric propeller with blades of narrow chord. The other two

Additional cowl flaps became a production standard beginning with the P-47D-1-RE. They were also retro-fitted to some earlier aircraft. At first, two additional flaps were added on each side. They were rectangular and had the same width as the other flaps as shown in this close-up. But on most aircraft, the two new flaps on each side were reduced in width along the trailing edge as shown in the top left photograph on page 49. *(USAFM)*

The Hamilton-Standard Hydromatic propeller was introduced on the P-47D-22-RE. This provided a considerable increase in performance, and the term "paddleblade" was used for the first time. Francis Gabreski once told the author that the Hamilton-Standard propeller allowed him to "walk away" from a Thunderbolt with the original Curtiss Electric prop. Here a P-47D-22-RE has its guns boresighted on specially designed targets in the distance. *(USAFM)*

The bubbletop canopy was first used on the P-47D-25-RE which was built at Farmingdale and fitted with Hamilton-Standard propellers. The P-47D-26-RA, which was the first bubbletop built at Evansville, had Curtiss Electric symmetrical paddleblade propellers. P-47D-27-REs like this one were essentially the same as the -26s, but they had Hamilton-Standard propellers. The red and white tail stripes on this aircraft indicate that it belongs to the 525th Fighter Squadron of the 86th Fighter Group. Also note that the serial number has been moved to the middle of the fuselage. (USAFM)

The P-47D-28-RA was produced with the asymmetrical Curtiss Electric propeller. Although added during production of the P-47D-40-RA, dorsal fins were often retrofitted to earlier aircraft to improve lateral stability which was lost when the spine of the fuselage was cut down for the bubble canopy. "Ponnie" was a P-47D-28-RA assigned to the 64th Fighter Squadron of the 57th Fighter Group within the 12th Air Force. (USAFM)

paddleblade propellers were built by Curtiss Electric, one having a symmetrical blade design and the other having a wider asymmetrical shape. These two Curtiss Electric paddleblade propellers were first installed on the P-47D-23-RA, which otherwise was the same as the P-47-22-RE. These two production blocks were also the last razorback Thunderbolts to be built.

The P-47D-25-RE at Farmingdale and the P-47D-26-RA at Evansville were the first to feature an electrically operated bubble canopy similar to that used on the British Hawker Typhoon. This meant that the classic razorback

rear fuselage had to be cut down, and a new windscreen was also installed. The improved visibility was important to the pilot in combat, but this change significantly altered the Jug's appearance. Thus began a debate as to which lines represented the "true" Thunderbolt; Kartveli's classic razorback or the sleeker bubbletop.

These two production blocks also saw an increase in internal fuel capacity from 305 gallons to 370 gallons to further extend the Thunderbolt's range. There were also changes in the cockpit layout, and the water tank for the

The P-47D-30-RE and -30-RA introduced compressibility flaps underneath each wing, just aft of the landing gear. This P-47D-30-RA was photographed by aviation author and photographer, Warren Bodie, at the Cleveland Air Races in 1948. By that time the designation had been changed to F-47, and this Thunderbolt was assigned to the District of Columbia Air National Guard. (Bodie)

The P-47D-40-RA was the first Thunderbolt to have a dorsal fin installed as a standard feature on the production line. The Mk. VIII gun sight was replaced with a K-14 sight, and provisions for zero-length launcher stubs for 5-inch rockets were installed in the wings. A tail warning radar was also added. This "Big Stud" was flown in the post-war years by Col. Robert Baseler. It carries markings similar to the ones used by Baseler when he was assigned to the 325th Fighter Group in Italy during 1944. (See the top right photo on page 7.) (Baseler via USAFM)

water injection system was increased to thirty gallons.

The next significant change occurred with the P-47D-30-RE and P-47D-30-RA when compressibility flaps were added under each wing at the 30-percent chord line just aft of the main gear doors. These were used to prevent an excessive buildup in speed during dives which made control and recovery difficult. A less noticeable change was that the ailerons had a blunt leading edge. Photographs indicate that many P-47D-30-REs and -RAs had a dorsal fin retrofitted in the field. This was the fin design that was installed during production on the P-47-40-RA. The P-47D-30-RE and -RA also had flat cockpit floors, while all previous Thunderbolts had corrugated floors.

The final production block in the D series was the P-47D-40-RA which had provisions for five zero-length rocket stubs under each wing. Kits to retrofit these rocket launchers to earlier D-models were supplied to the field, but most U. S. Thunderbolts used the 4.5-inch triple tube launchers when rockets were required for a mission. The P-47-40-RA also had a dorsal fin installed on the production line, and a tail warning radar was also standard. The K-14 gun sight replaced the Mk. VIII.

Model P-47D
Number built 12,602

Data below for: P-47D-28-RE

ENGINE . . . . P&W R-2800-59

PERFORMANCE
Max Speed/Altitude . . . . . . 428 mph/30,000 feet
Cruising Speed . . . . 340 mph
Max Range/Altitude . . . . 1,030 miles/10,000 feet
Normal Range/Altitude . . . 590 miles/25,000 feet
Service Ceiling . . . . 42,000 feet
Climb . . . . 6.2 minutes to 15,000 feet

WEIGHTS
Empty . . . . 10,000 pounds
Gross . . . . 14,500 pounds
Max Take off . . . . 17,500 pounds

DIMENSIONS
Span . . . . 40 feet, 9.25 inches
Wing Area . . . . 300 square feet
Length . . . . 36 feet, 1.75 inches
Height . . . . 14 feet, 8 inches

FUEL
Internal . . . . 370 gallons
External . . . . 410 gallons

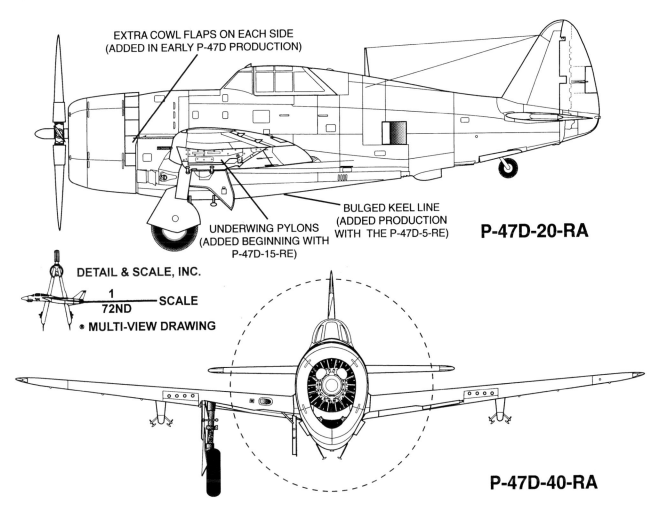

EXTRA COWL FLAPS ON EACH SIDE
(ADDED IN EARLY P-47D PRODUCTION)

BULGED KEEL LINE
(ADDED PRODUCTION
WITH THE P-47D-5-RE)

UNDERWING PYLONS
(ADDED BEGINNING WITH
P-47D-15-RE)

P-47D-20-RA

DETAIL & SCALE, INC.

1
———— SCALE
72ND

® MULTI-VIEW DRAWING

P-47D-40-RA

DETAIL & SCALE 1/72nd SCALE COPYRIGHT © DRAWINGS BY LLOYD S. JONES

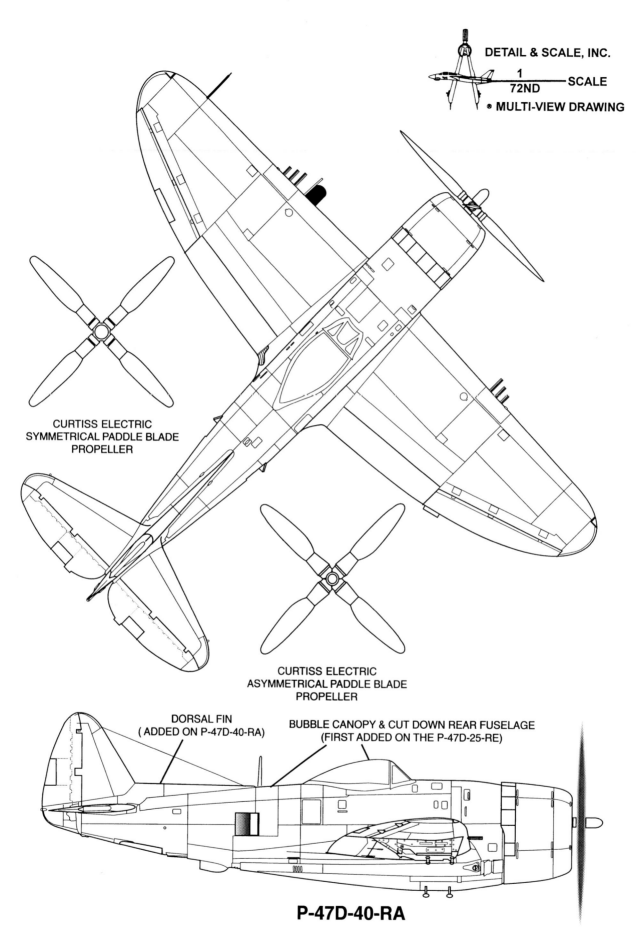

DETAIL & SCALE, INC.

$\dfrac{1}{72\text{ND}}$ ——— SCALE

● MULTI-VIEW DRAWING

CURTISS ELECTRIC
SYMMETRICAL PADDLE BLADE
PROPELLER

CURTISS ELECTRIC
ASYMMETRICAL PADDLE BLADE
PROPELLER

DORSAL FIN
(ADDED ON P-47D-40-RA)

BUBBLE CANOPY & CUT DOWN REAR FUSELAGE
(FIRST ADDED ON THE P-47D-25-RE)

P-47D-40-RA

DETAIL & SCALE 1/72nd SCALE COPYRIGHT © DRAWINGS BY LLOYD S. JONES

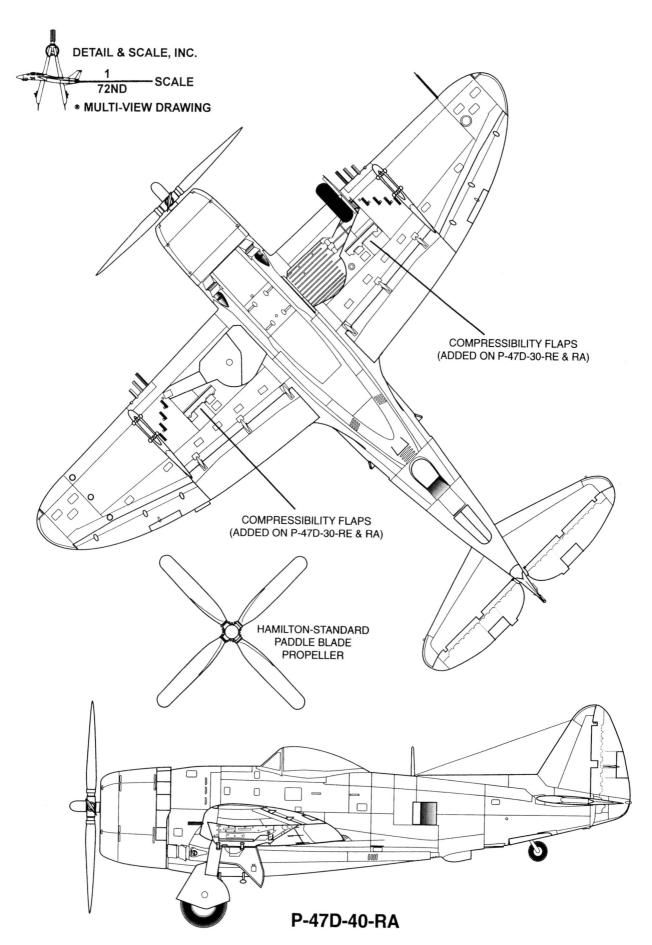

DETAIL & SCALE, INC.

$\dfrac{1}{72ND}$ ——— SCALE

® MULTI-VIEW DRAWING

COMPRESSIBILITY FLAPS
(ADDED ON P-47D-30-RE & RA)

COMPRESSIBILITY FLAPS
(ADDED ON P-47D-30-RE & RA)

HAMILTON-STANDARD
PADDLE BLADE
PROPELLER

P-47D-40-RA

DETAIL & SCALE 1/72nd SCALE COPYRIGHT © DRAWINGS BY LLOYD S. JONES

P-47D DETAILS

CANOPY DETAILS

The windscreen used with the standard framed canopy was simple in design yet quite efficient, because it created very little drag.

Although this restored Thunderbolt at the U. S. Air Force Museum is painted to represent a P-47D-15-RA, it is actually a Curtiss built P-47G. P-47Gs were used only for training and other non-combat duties, and therefore they were often lacking standard combat equipment. In this case, the flat bulletproof glass and the gun sight under the windscreen are not present.

An overall view of the framed canopy used on razorback Thunderbolts illustrates how the pilot's visibility was restricted by the framework and the high razorback spine of the aircraft.

The concave area of the spine just aft of the seat was designed to provide some rearward view through the aft pane of glass on each side. However, this proved to be very limited, and pilots often relied more on mirrors mounted above the windscreen to check their six o'clock position.

The framed canopy is shown in the completely open position. The P-47's framed canopy was considered better than that on the P-51 Mustang (through the P-51C variant), because it slid aft and afforded access to the cockpit from both sides. The P-51's framed canopy opened only from the left side.

A few razorback P-47s were fitted with the semi-bubble Malcolm hood canopy, however this was done far less often than it was on P-51B and P-51C Mustangs. This particular Thunderbolt was assigned to the 5th Emergency Rescue Squadron. "War Weary" P-47s were sometimes assigned to this important support role after their combat days were over.   (Brown/USAF via Ethell and Bell)

Realizing the importance of seeing the enemy first in both offensive and defensive aerial combat, bubble canopies replaced framed designs on many allied fighter types. The P-47 was no exception, and the bubble canopy shown here became standard on the P-47D-25-RE and the P-47D-26-RA. This changed the overall appearance of the aircraft considerably, but more importantly it increased the pilot's visibility by a significant margin.

The canopy slid aft on rails on each side of the cockpit, and there was a slot along the top of the fuselage just aft of the seat. A brace, fitted between the canopy's lower framework, had a center guide that traveled inside this slot as the canopy moved forward and aft.

This close-up provides a better look at the sliding bubble canopy and its framework.

The windscreen used with the bubble canopy was completely different than that used with the earlier framed design. The front flat glass was bulletproof to provide protection for the pilot.

With no spine on the aircraft, a different type of rear protection had to be provided for the pilot. Armor plate was placed just behind the seat to protect the pilot's head and shoulders. This view also provides another look at the center slot and brace.

PROPELLERS

Other references on the P-47 have stated that there were three types of propellers used operationally on the Thunderbolt, but in fact there were four. The first was this thin-blade Curtiss Electric propeller. *(USAFM)*

A Hamilton-Standard Hydromatic propeller, with a diameter of 13' 1 7/8 inches, was introduced on the P-47D-22-RE, and it continued to be used on some subsequent production blocks built at Farmingdale. It had blades with a broader chord, and the use of the term "paddleblade" became common. *(USAFM)*

The original Curtiss Electric propeller had a diameter of 12' 2" and was fitted to all production Thunderbolts up through the P-47D-21-RA. This close-up provides a good look at the blade's design and its rather pointed tip.

The blades of the Hamilton-Standard Hydromatic propeller were cuffless, and the tips were more rounded than on the earlier Curtiss Electric propellers. The markings, including the Hamilton Standard logo, can be seen here. *(Roeder)*

The hub of the Hamilton-Standard propeller was shorter and considerably less pointed than on any of the Curtiss Electric props. *(Graser)*

Above: Curtiss Electric also introduced two different propellers with wider chords, and these were first used in production on the P-47D-23-RA. One design looked very much like the Hamilton-Standard Hydromatic propeller, except that it was fitted with cuffs. This propeller was known generally as the Curtiss Electric symmetrical paddleblade propeller, and it was 13' 1" in diameter.
(USAFM)

Right: This close-up provides a good look at one of the blades on a Curtiss Electric symmetrical paddleblade propeller.

Above: The other Curtiss Electric paddleblade was asymmetrical, because the broadening of the blade's chord was much more pronounced along the trailing edge. Like the symmetrical propeller, it was also 13' 1" in diameter. Most published drawings of this propeller show this feature incorrectly, because they do not illustrate that the broadening of the trailing edge tapers as it approaches the tip rather than remaining almost constant.   (USAFM)

Right: Here is a close-up of the asymmetrical Curtiss Electric paddleblade propeller. Note that it was a cuffed design, as were all Curtiss Electric props used on the Thunderbolt. It should be noted that although some P-47 production blocks were fitted with a certain type of propeller, there was considerable changing of propellers in the field. Even some of the earlier P-47Bs, -Cs, and -Ds were sometimes retrofitted with one of the three paddleblade props.

LANDING GEAR DETAILS

RIGHT MAIN LANDING GEAR

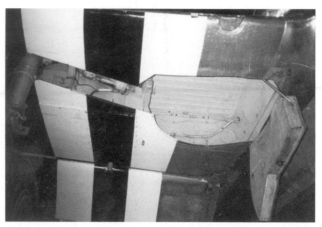

More details can be seen in this view that looks aft into the right main gear well. The interior of the wheel wells on Thunderbolts were painted Chromate Yellow on the Republic production lines. Chromate Green was sometimes applied in the field, and this color was also used on Curtiss built P-47Gs.

Although there were some minor changes, the design of the Thunderbolt's landing gear remained essentially the same for all production variants except the P-47N. This is a look at the right main landing gear. There were six spokes on the wheel, but quite often a flat disc was attached to cover the entire inner side of the wheel.

The inner main gear doors hung down vertically next to the fuselage.

The outer portion of the right main gear well is visible here. The hydraulic cylinder that actuated the main gear strut for retraction and extension can be seen in the narrow portion of the well just inboard of the main strut.

A smaller hydraulic cylinder operated the inner main gear door. It can be seen here along the front of the right main gear well.

LEFT MAIN LANDING GEAR

This front view illustrates that, when extended, the strut was perpendicular to the wing, not to the ground. Also note how the two main outer gear doors overlap at the oleo. The interior surfaces of these doors were painted Chromate Yellow by Republic and Chromate Green by Curtiss.

There was a small flap at the top of the upper outer gear door where it met the fuselage. It closed over an opening between the door and the wing when the gear was retracted.

The interior of the left main gear well is shown here.

The shapes of the outer doors can be seen in this outside view of the left main landing gear.

This is the inner door on the left main gear of a P-47D.

TAIL LANDING GEAR

When retracted, the tail wheel was covered by two doors. It was mounted on a single strut that entered on the left side of the wheel. This is the right side of the airplane, but because it was pushed back into a parked position, the tail wheel has castored around, and the left side of the wheel and strut is visible.

The door on the left side is shown here, but this is the right side of the tail wheel.

This view looks up and aft into the tail wheel well. On operational aircraft, the inside surfaces of the doors and the inside of the well were painted Chromate Yellow on Republic built Thunderbolts, and Chromate Green on those built by Curtiss. Again, the tail wheel assembly is castored around 180 degrees in this photo.

After raising the tail of the plane up on jacks, it was possible to take this photograph which looks up into the tail wheel well of a P-47D which was under restoration. The arms which open and close the tail wheel doors are visible. The tail gear well was often covered by a protective fabric boot on operational aircraft.

Coverage of P-47D details continues on page 49.

COLOR GALLERY
P-47 INSIGNIAS & STANDARD MARKINGS

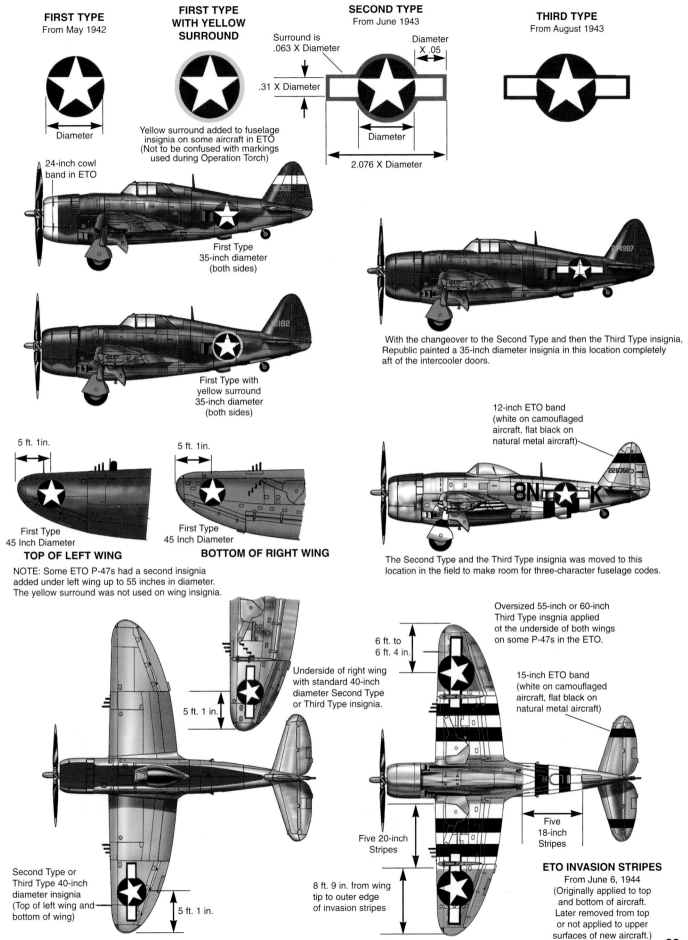

FIRST TYPE
From May 1942

Diameter

FIRST TYPE WITH YELLOW SURROUND

Yellow surround added to fuselage insignia on some aircraft in ETO (Not to be confused with markings used during Operation Torch)

SECOND TYPE
From June 1943

Surround is .063 X Diameter

Diameter X .05

.31 X Diameter

Diameter

2.076 X Diameter

THIRD TYPE
From August 1943

24-inch cowl band in ETO

First Type
35-inch diameter
(both sides)

First Type with yellow surround
35-inch diameter
(both sides)

With the changeover to the Second Type and then the Third Type insignia, Republic painted a 35-inch diameter insignia in this location completely aft of the intercooler doors.

5 ft. 1in.

First Type
45 Inch Diameter
TOP OF LEFT WING

5 ft. 1in.

First Type
45 Inch Diameter
BOTTOM OF RIGHT WING

NOTE: Some ETO P-47s had a second insignia added under left wing up to 55 inches in diameter. The yellow surround was not used on wing insignia.

12-inch ETO band (white on camouflaged aircraft, flat black on natural metal aircraft)

8N + K

The Second Type and the Third Type insignia was moved to this location in the field to make room for three-character fuselage codes.

Underside of right wing with standard 40-inch diameter Second Type or Third Type insignia.

5 ft. 1 in.

Second Type or Third Type 40-inch diameter insignia (Top of left wing and bottom of wing)

5 ft. 1 in.

Oversized 55-inch or 60-inch Third Type insignia applied ot the underside of both wings on some P-47s in the ETO.

15-inch ETO band (white on camouflaged aircraft, flat black on natural metal aircraft)

6 ft. to 6 ft. 4 in.

Five 20-inch Stripes

Five 18-inch Stripes

8 ft. 9 in. from wing tip to outer edge of invasion stripes

ETO INVASION STRIPES
From June 6, 1944
(Originally applied to top and bottom of aircraft. Later removed from top or not applied to upper surfaces of new aircraft.)

33

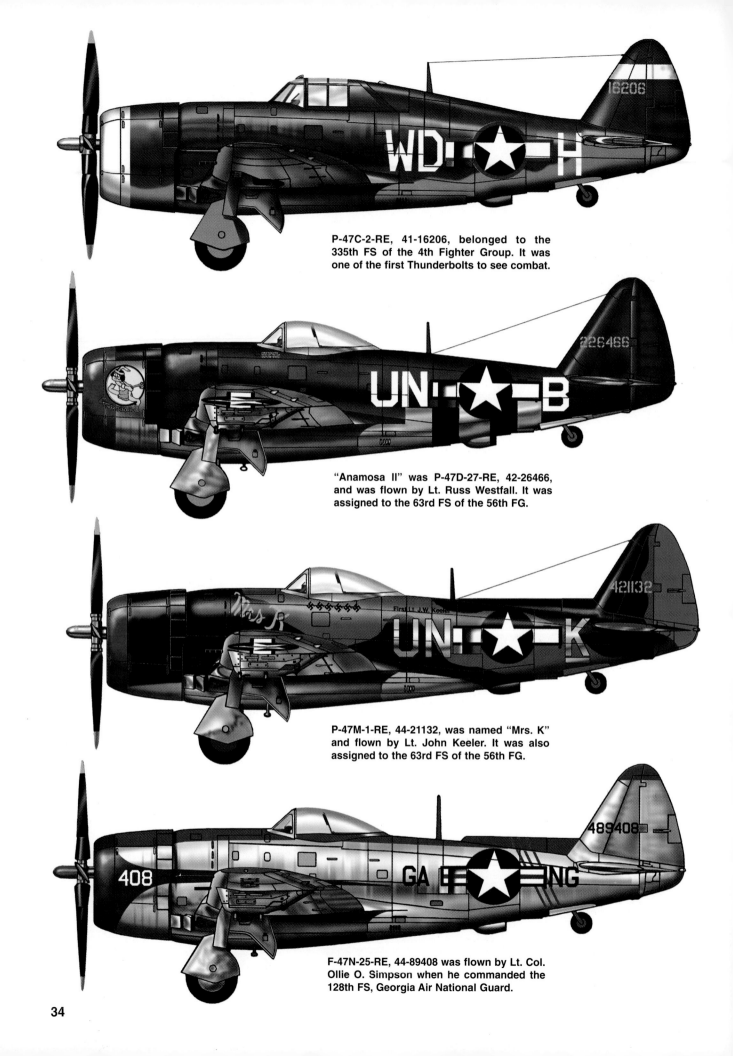

P-47C-2-RE, 41-16206, belonged to the 335th FS of the 4th Fighter Group. It was one of the first Thunderbolts to see combat.

"Anamosa II" was P-47D-27-RE, 42-26466, and was flown by Lt. Russ Westfall. It was assigned to the 63rd FS of the 56th FG.

P-47M-1-RE, 44-21132, was named "Mrs. K" and flown by Lt. John Keeler. It was also assigned to the 63rd FS of the 56th FG.

F-47N-25-RE, 44-89408 was flown by Lt. Col. Ollie O. Simpson when he commanded the 128th FS, Georgia Air National Guard.

WORLD WAR II COLORS & MARKINGS

Above: Early Thunderbolts were often assigned to various training units. These aircraft commonly had painted designs on the cowling like that shown here on a P-47C. While originally painted Olive Drab over Neutral Gray, this aircraft shows signs of patchy repainting with a darker green color. Also note the Chromate Yellow primer on the inside of the main gear door. (USAAF via Bell)

Right: "Gloria" was a P-47D assigned to the 348th Fighter Group of the 5th Air Force in the Pacific. The leading edge of the wing was painted white as was the tail section. The yellow tip on the vertical tail indicates the 341st Fighter Squadron. (Kuhn via Bell)

Below: Markings of the 91st FS of the 81st FG are displayed on this P-47D. It was not uncommon to see natural metal drop tanks on Thunderbolts, although many were painted Neutral Gray. (Via Bell)

Above: Although the Olive Drab over Neutral Gray camouflage and the natural metal finish were the only two official schemes specified for Thunderbolts, some units, particularly the 56th Fighter Group, painted a number of unofficial camouflage schemes on their aircraft. This included a wide variety of colors throughout the war, but British greens, grays, and blues were common. What appears to be flak damage on the tail of this P-47D-22-RE is actually natural metal showing through where the paint has worn away. This Thunderbolt, coded UN*B, was flown by Lt. Cameron Hart, an ace with six kills.

(Graser collection)

Below: Natural metal Thunderbolts in the 56th FG seem to be more of the exception than the rule. But "Pat," a P-47D-28-RA, was one of these exceptions. The 56th FG even camouflaged most of its P-47Ms right up to the end of the war. (Graser collection)

Dark green has been applied in an irregular pattern on the upper and vertical surfaces of this Thunderbolt which is otherwise painted in the standard Olive Drab over Neutral Gray scheme. This aircraft is a P-47D-11-RE named "GIORGI." Note also how the dark green has been used to paint over the invasion stripes on the upper fuselage and the top of the wings of this aircraft, as well as on the one in the photograph above. This color is also used on the top of the nose section as well. (Graser collection)

Above: The first Air Commando Group, which was part of the 10th Air Force in the Pacific, had used diagonal white stripes for identification on its camouflaged aircraft. However, the stripes were changed to black on natural metal aircraft as illustrated on this P-47D-23-RA. Loop antennas were common on aircraft which operated in the China-India-Burma theater.   (via Ethell and Bell)

Left: "Juicy Lucy" was assigned to the 313th Fighter Squadron of the 50th Fighter Group, and it was flown by Phil Savides. This unit was part of the 9th Air Force in Europe. While nose art was most often seen on the left side of the aircraft, it was not uncommon to see it on the right or both sides of Thunderbolts. In this case, it was only on the left. Note the Hamilton-Standard propeller on this P-47D-26-RA.   (Savides via Graser)

Below (both photos): A P-47N-1-RE has its guns bore-sighted on Ie Shima late in the war. The blue cowl and tail markings are those used by the 19th Fighter Squadron of the 318th Fighter Group.   (Graser collection)

U. S. AIR FORCE THUNDERBOLTS

Above: P-47Ds and P-47Ns continued to serve in the post-war years with the U. S. Army Air Forces. In 1947, when the U. S. Air Force was established, remaining Thunderbolts were redesignated F-47Ds and F-47Ns. The red bar was added to the national insignia in 1948. This F-47D is painted in the markings of the 525th Fighter Bomber Squadron of the 86th Fighter Bomber Group.
(Crain via Menard)

Below: This F-47N has the simple markings of the 332nd Fighter Group. Because there were no unit codes, the national insignia on the fuselage sides were usually painted aft of the intercooler doors during the post-war years. (Larkings via Menard)

These F-47Ns belong to the 81st Fighter Group in Hawaii. It appears that this unit adopted the tail markings that had been used on P-47Ds of the 79th Fighter Group in Italy during World War II. These markings consisted of a blue tail with yellow lightning bolts. (Satterfield via Menard)

AIR NATIONAL GUARD THUNDERBOLTS

Above: Air National Guard units also flew F-47Ds and F-47Ns during the post-war era. These F-47Ds were assigned to the Virginia Air National Guard. The Virginia Guard continued a Republic tradition by later flying the F-84 and F-105. (Larkins via Menard)

Middle: This F-47D carries the markings of the District of Columbia Air National Guard. Note the commander's stripes around the fuselage. The location of the fuselage insignia on Guard Thunderbolts varied considerably and often were simply positioned so that they would fit between the abbreviation for the state and the ANG lettering. (Menard collection)

Right: An immaculate F-47N from the Delaware Guard has nothing to indicate its unit except the lettering on the sides of the fuselage. Post-war Thunderbolts were often painted with silver dope which helped to seal the skin and prevent corrosion.
(Boseth via Menard)

P-47D COCKPIT DETAILS & COLORS

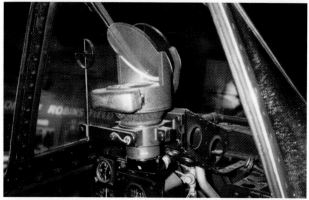

Above: P-47D-30-RA, 44-32691, was in service at what is now Robins Air Force Base when it was taken off the line and placed directly in storage for the Museum of Aviation in Warner Robins, Georgia. All details in the cockpit, including the Dark Dull Green color, remain exactly as they were when the aircraft was in service. This makes the photographs on this page and the next very valuable as a historical record of the Thunderbolt's cockpit, because no restoration work has been done. This is the instrument panel as viewed from the left side.

Left: Details of the reflector gun sight are visible here. Note also the back-up ring sight mounted on the reflector unit.

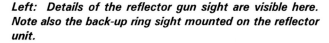

The left side of the cockpit is shown here. The throttle quadrant and electrical distribution box are the major items on this side along with the trim wheels.

The right side of the cockpit was less cluttered. Thunderbolts built by both Republic lines left the factory with cockpits painted Dull Dark Green rather than Chromate Green as used by Curtiss.

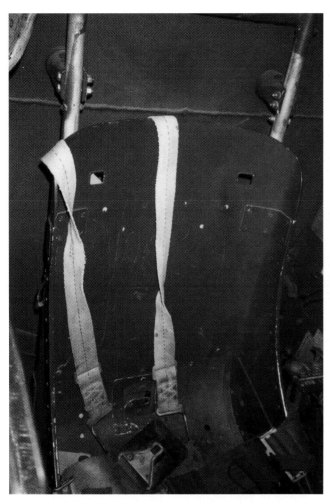

The seat was also painted the *Dull Dark Green* color. Note that the shoulder straps are off-white, while the lap belts are khaki.

The top of the pilot's armor and head rest are visible here. The head rest was often black as shown here, but in other cases it could be brown or gray.

The bottom of the seat can be seen in this view. The pilot sat on his parachute which also served as a cushion in the seat bucket.

The control column and the rudder pedals were also *Dull Dark Green*. Note that the floor is smooth rather than being corrugated.

P-47G COCKPIT DETAILS & COLORS

Above: Although the exterior is painted to represent a P-47D, this Thunderbolt, which is on display at the USAF Museum in Dayton, Ohio, is actually a Curtiss built P-47G. Curtiss used Chromate Green primer for the cockpit interior instead of the Dull Dark Green used by Republic. This photograph shows details of the instrument panel which remains almost completely intact.

The top of the control column can be seen here.

The rudder pedals are illustrated in this view. Note the corrugated floor as compared to smooth floor in the P-47D-30-RA on the previous two pages.

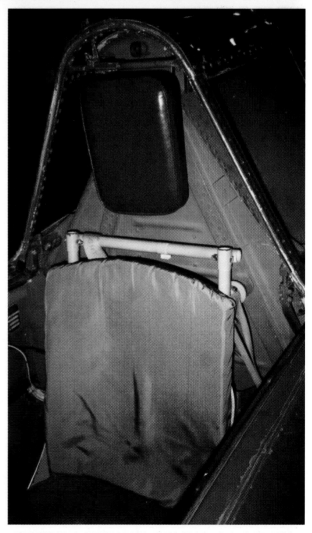

The design for the head rest and pilot's armor was different in the razorback Thunderbolts than on the later bubbletops.

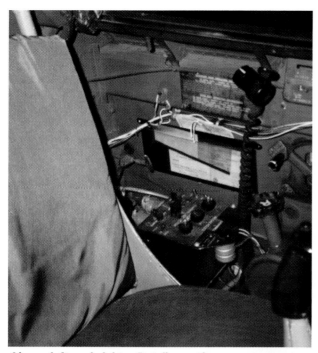

Above left and right: Details on the left side of the P-47G's cockpit are illustrated in these two photographs. The cockpit in most P-47Gs was almost identical to those in Republic built P-47D-10-RE razorbacks except for the color of the paint.

Right: A close-up provides a good look at the throttle, control column, and the electrical distribution panel.

Below left and right: The right side of the cockpit in all Thunderbolts was relatively simple and uncluttered.

P-47M COCKPIT DETAILS & COLORS

The instrument panel in the P-47M was very similar to that in late P-47Ds.

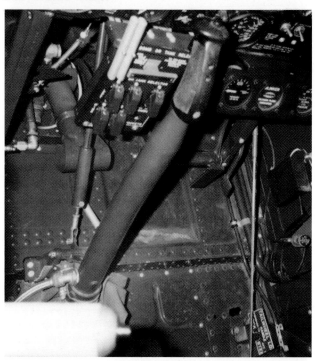

The Yanks Air Museum in Chino, California, has a beautifully restored P-47M-1-RE. The paint used in the cockpit matches what factory fresh Dull Dark Green would have looked like.

The floor in the P-47M was without corrugations like that in late P-47Ds.

Most items on the sides of the cockpit also remain as they had been on late P-47Ds.

P-47N COCKPIT DETAILS & COLORS

The instrument panel remains as it was when the P-47N-25-RE was in service with the Air National Guard, but the gun sight has been removed.

One of the few remaining P-47Ns is on display at the excellent USAF Armament Museum. It was last used operationally by the Air National Guard, and many Guard aircraft had cockpits that were painted black. This is true for this Thunderbolt, and only the floor and rudder pedals remain Chromate Green as applied at a depot.

The left side of the cockpit was essentially unchanged from that in P-47Ds and P-47Ms. However, note that the seat in the P-47N had arm rests to relieve fatigue on long range flights. This feature was added during production of the P-47N-15-RE.

The top of the seat and pilot's armor were also painted black.

The right side of the cockpit had a number of differences when compared to earlier Thunderbolts, but the usual map and documents holder can be seen next to the seat. Again, note the padded arm rest in this photo.

R-2800 ENGINE DETAILS & COLORS

This Pratt & Whitney R-2800-21 engine was used in the P-47B, but the powerplant used in Thunderbolts up through the last of the P-47Ds had only detail differences. Noteworthy is the smooth rounded reduction gear housing. The R-2800 also powered the F6F Hellcat and F4U Corsair fighters.

Features on the aft end of the engine can be seen in this view.

Right side details of the engine are illustrated here.

The accessory compartment was directly behind the engine. This is the right side of the compartment on a P-47D-40-RA.

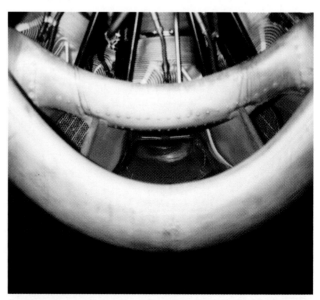

Carburetion and cooling air entered through an air scoop just below the engine in the Thunderbolt's huge cowling. Note the dividers inside the scoop.

The R-2800-57 "C-series" engines used in the P-47M and P-47N had a different appearance when viewed from the front. The reduction gear housing was larger, more cylindrical in shape, and it was covered with numerous bolts. Compare this to the earlier engine seen on the previous page.

The rear of the R-2800-57 is shown here.

Left and right side views provide a look at more details on the R-2800-57 powerplant.

GUN BAY DETAILS & COLORS

This well known photo of armorers loading ammunition for the left side guns on Gabreski's Thunderbolt is included for comparison purposes. Republic painted the interior of the gun bays with Chromate Yellow primer as can be seen here. **(USAAF via Bell)**

The .50-caliber ammunition was loaded in four parallel trays outboard of the guns. **(Ethell)**

Curtiss used Chromate Green primer in the gun bays, and it was sometimes used on Republic built Thunderbolts at field depots. It can be seen here in this overall view of the left gun bay in a restored P-47D-40-RA. **(Ethell)**

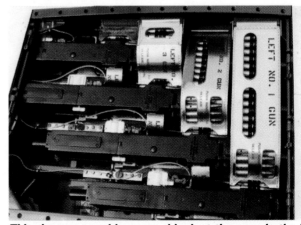

This close-up provides a good look at the guns in the left wing. All details are correct and as they would be in an operational P-47. The guns in the right wing would be a mirror image of what is shown here. **(Ethell)**

FUSELAGE DETAILS

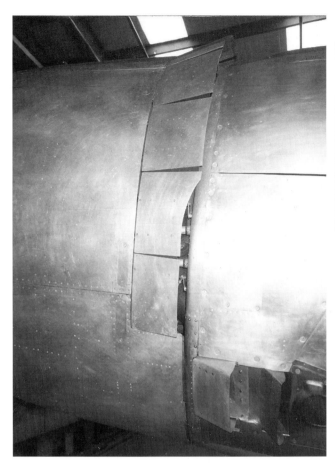

P-47Bs, P-47Cs, and some early P-47Ds had cowl flaps which extended only down to the centerline of the fuselage. But most Thunderbolts had two additional flaps below the centerline on each side as shown here. Note the shape of the two lower flaps. When first installed, these were rectangular, but on most Thunderbolts, they were reduced in width as illustrated here.

A bulged keel line with a shackle and plumbing for an external drop tank became a production standard with the P-47D-5-RE. This feature was also retrofitted to some earlier Thunderbolts through the use of kits installed in the field. The fittings and anti-sway braces can be seen in this right front view.

A movable oil cooler control door was located on each side of the forward fuselage. An exhaust waste gate was located aft of it, and a deflector was between the door and the waste gate. This is the arrangement on the left side. It should be noted that the deflector was not present on P-47Bs or early P-47Cs without the eight-inch forward fuselage extension.

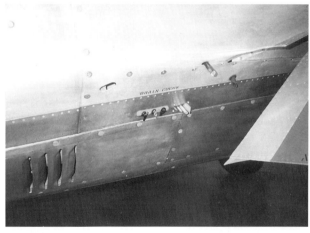

Drain cocks were located just aft of the right wing root. A little further aft were the central fuselage cooling louvers.

A hoist tube ran all the way through the aft fuselage. It was used to lift the rear of the aircraft for maintenance and for boresighting the guns.

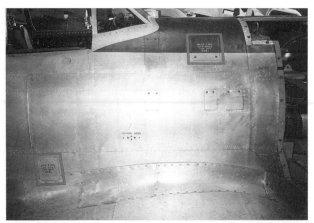

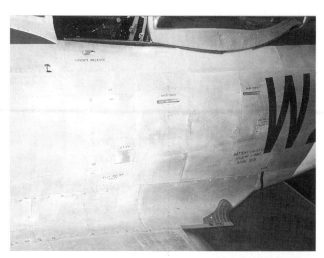

Several features on the right side of the fuselage can be seen here. The filler for the main fuel tank is beneath a panel which is outlined in red near the top of the fuselage. The auxiliary fuel tank filler was beneath another panel just above the wing root. It too is outlined in red. A grounding point, consisting of a series of small holes, is also visible above the wing root.

On the left side of the center fuselage is a canopy release just below the canopy rail. There is a flap covered step about mid-way up on the side of the fuselage, and a swing out hand hold is just above it and to the right. Also note the reinforced step area on the wing filet.

A boarding step was just behind the left wing root, and below it were the left center fuselage louvers.

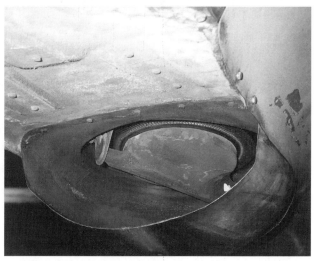

The antenna wire began at a point near the top of the vertical tail and entered the fuselage just to the right of the antenna mast.

Details of the turbosupercharger can be seen inside its shroud beneath the aft fuselage.

INTERCOOLER DOORS

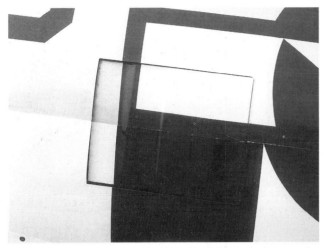

There has been much confusion about how the intercooler doors worked on the sides of the fuselage. Did they slide forward or open out? Actually, they did both as shown in the sequence of photographs on this page. This view shows the left door fully closed. Note how the markings line up with the door in this position. *(Graser)*

As Jeff Ethell sits in the cockpit and operates the doors, Norris Graser continues the photography of the operation. Here the door has moved slightly forward as can be seen by how much the insignia and invasion stripes are offset between the fuselage and the door. But the door has not yet started to open. *(Graser)*

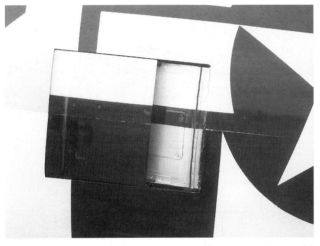

As the door continues forward, it still remains flush with the fuselage. Note how the forward vertical bar of the insignia has now disappeared from view. *(Graser)*

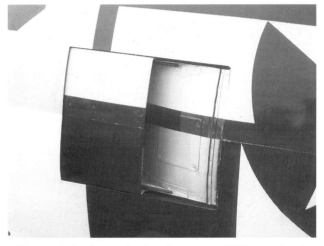

More of the inner ducting becomes visible as the door continues to slide forward. Note how the insignia is also painted on the inner ducting. *(Graser)*

Only when the door reaches this point does it finally begin to open outward slightly from the fuselage. *(Graser)*

From a point further aft, the interior of the fully opened door is revealed.

WING DETAILS

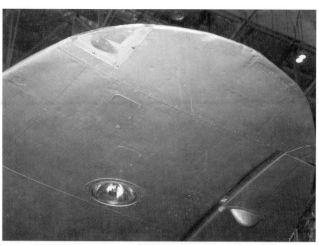

On all production Thunderbolts except the P-47N-25-RE, the navigation lights on the wing tips were located under a clear triangular covering at the end of the leading edge. A teardrop-shaped lens of the appropriate color was under the clear cover. This is the green light on the right wing tip, although the color actually appears to be blue.

The red light on the left wing tip is shown here. Also note the retractable landing/taxi light under the wing. Many Thunderbolts had the landing/taxi light located in this position. In other cases, it was further inboard as illustrated below.

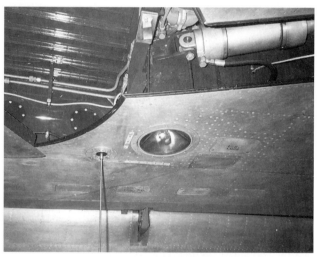

Three identification lights were located under the right wing near the tip. They were red, green, and amber from front to rear. However, the middle light appeared to be blue rather than green.

Some Thunderbolts had the landing/taxi light located just behind the left main gear well as shown here. The whip antenna on this restored aircraft was not on operational P-47s.

Cooling air for the cockpit was taken into the aircraft through an oval air scoop which was on the leading edge of the right wing. A little further outboard was the gun camera with its small rectangular lens.

The pitot probe was mounted on the leading edge of the left wing near the tip.

The right flap is shown here in the partially lowered position. A red "NO STEP" area was usually painted on the top of both flaps near the inboard end, and it overlapped on to the wing at the root.

This is the same flap shown at left as viewed from below. The three large hinges are clearly visible.

There was a fixed balance tab at the inboard end of the right aileron. The stencilling on it reads, "TAB ADJUSTED AT FACTORY, DO NOT TOUCH."

The adjustable trim tab on the left aileron could be controlled from the cockpit. There was no adjustable trim tab on the right aileron.

This underside view of the left aileron reveals the three hinges with their fairings. The adjustable trim tab is visible in a slightly down position.

COMPRESSIBILITY FLAPS

The heavy Thunderbolt could reach 600 miles-per-hour in dives, and this led to compressibility problems. Compressibility flaps were introduced on the P-47D-30-RA and RE, and they were located just aft of the gear well under each wing. This is the compressibility flap under the right wing, and it is in the open position.

When closed, the compressibility flaps stood proud of the surrounding wing and looked a lot like a reinforcing panel. This is the flap under the left wing in the closed position.

Above and right: The open compressibility flap under the left wing is shown from the front in the photograph above, and from the rear in the photo to the right. Also note the three actuators in the close-up at right.

PYLONS

Beginning with the production of the P-47D-15-RE, the wings were strengthened to carry external fuel tanks and bombs on pylons. These pylons remained standard on all subsequent P-47Ds, -Ms, and -Ns, and they were retrofitted to some earlier aircraft. This is the pylon under the right wing as viewed from the outside.

The pylon under the left wing can be seen here. The pylons were removable and were often not carried on P-47Ms.

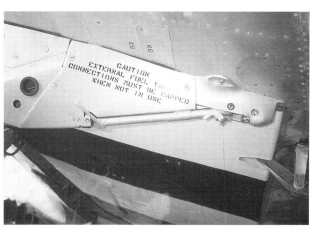

At the aft end of the pylon was a stabilization bar that was stowed in this position when not in use.

A front view provides a good look at the anti-sway braces.

The bar could be rotated down around a hinge on its aft end to provide bracing for an external fuel tank.

TAIL DETAILS

VERTICAL TAIL

The wire antenna was attached to the leading edge of the vertical tail at this point.

Rudders on P-47Bs were originally covered with fabric, but this was changed to a metal-skinned rudder on all subsequent Thunderbolts.

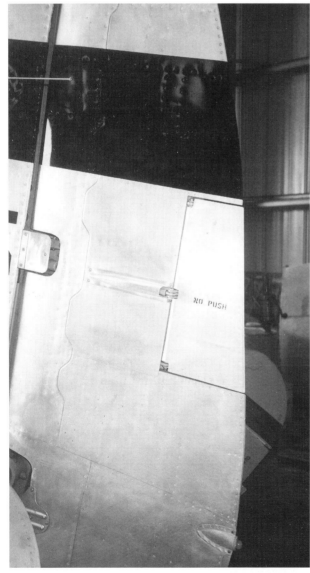

The trim tab on the rudder is shown here from the left side along with the fairing that covered its actuator.

A white position light was located on the trailing edge of the rudder near the bottom.

HORIZONTAL TAIL

Like the rudder, original elevators were covered with fabric, but this was changed to metal-skinned elevators by the time the first P-47C was produced. The entire right horizontal tail can be seen in this view.

The left horizontal tail is shown here. Two covered hinges attached the elevator to the horizontal stabilizer.

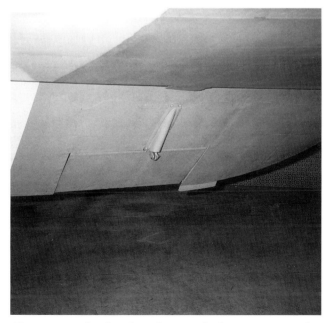

The actuator for the trim tab on each elevator was on the undersurface.

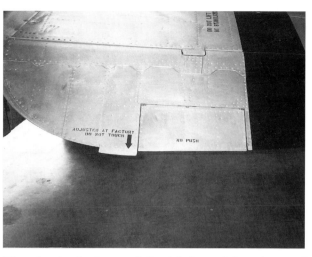

The elevator had a small fixed balance tab and a much larger adjustable trim tab on the trailing edge.

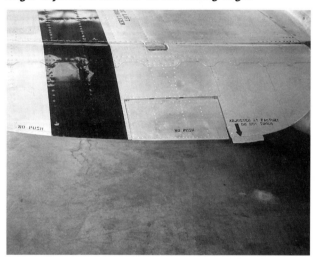

As with the right elevator, the left elevator also had both fixed and adjustable tabs.

This is the leading edge of the right stabilizer at the tip. Note that there is a small tab with a hole in it attached where the leading edge curves around to the tip. Another identical tab was located in the same place on the left stabilizer. A wire antenna could be attached to each with the opposite end of the wire antenna entering the side of the fuselage forward of the intercooler doors. This provision appears to be on almost all Thunderbolts, although the author has never seen these wire antennas in pictures of operational P-47s.

57

EXTERNAL STORES

After the bulged keel was added to the P-47, external tanks could be carried under the fuselage. Occasionally, bombs were also loaded on the centerline station. The strengthened wings permitted tanks and other stores to be carried under the wings. The small tank under the fuselage of this Thunderbolt had a capacity of seventy-five gallons. This tank was also used on the wing pylons. The larger tanks on the pylons each contained 165 gallons of fuel, but this size tank was too large to be mounted under the fuselage. *(USAFM)*

The centerline tank on this aircraft is an early tank made of impregnated paper. Paper tanks were all similar in appearance, but different sizes were available. Capacities ranged from 105 to 200 gallons. Five hundred-pound bombs are loaded on the wing pylons. This aircraft was flown by Captain Pat Pardridge who was assigned to the 23rd Fighter Squadron of the 36th Fighter Group. The photo was taken in October 1944. *(USAFM)*

In addition to fuel tanks and bombs, smoke generation units were also carried by Thunderbolts. *(USAFM)*

Until the development of the P-47D-40-RA, rocket stubs were not mounted under the wings of Thunderbolts. When rocket armament was required on earlier P-47s, they were usually fitted with triple tube launchers for 4.5-inch rockets. These devices were mounted directly below the guns under each wing, and the pylons remained free to carry other stores. *(USAFM)*

The British used rocket rails under the wings of their Thunderbolts. *(USAFM)*

P-47G

Above: The P-47G was built by Curtiss in five different production blocks. A total of 354 were built over a period of about two years, and two of these were converted to two-seat trainers. P-47Gs did not have pylons under the wings, and they often did not have full combat equipment. Production problems plagued the P-47G, and quality control was substandard. None were ever used in combat. Instead, they were used only in training and test programs. (USAFM)

Right: P-40 Warhawks roll down the assembly line at the Curtiss plant, but in the background, P-47Gs can be seen on a parallel line. (USAFM)

Left: Early P-47G-1-CUs like this one were comparable to the first Republic built P-47Cs. Note the original cowl flap design on this aircraft. With each of the five production blocks, improvements were added to the Curtiss built Thunderbolts, so that the last block of P-47G-15-CU aircraft was similar to the P-47D-10-RE. (USAFM)

Below, left and right: This P-47G-1-CU was used to test a landing gear with skis. (Both USAFM)

EXPERIMENTAL THUNDERBOLTS

The XP-47F was modified from a P-47B airframe (41-5938) to test a wing with a laminar-flow airfoil on the Thunderbolt. This was known as Project MX-116, and it was carried out in August 1942. Tests were conducted at Wright Field, Ohio, and by NACA at Langley Field, Virginia. Although the laminar-flow wing proved very successful with the P-51, no further development came from the XP-47F project. Note the original fabric-covered rudder on this aircraft.   (USAFM)

Two P-47D-15-RA airframes (42-23279 and 42-23298) were modified to be powered by the Chrysler IV-2220-11/GE engine with a CH-5 supercharger. These aircraft were given the XP-47H designation. The first of the two test aircraft is shown here in its original configuration. Note the oval shaped hole on the side of the aft fuselage. This hole, and the one on the opposite side of the fuselage, proved inadequate in providing air to the compressor.   (USAFM)

Above: The oval shaped holes were later covered with air scoops as seen in this flying shot of the same aircraft. While these improved air flow to the compressor, their drag caused a decrease in top speed.   (USAFM)

Left: Workers pose with an XP-47H. Note the cuffless Curtiss Electric propeller and the open panels revealing some features of the engine which produced 2500 horsepower at 3400 rpm for take off. Top speed was in excess of 400 miles-per-hour, and the ceiling was 36,000 feet. Many other aircraft designs were tested with exotic engine developments, but as with the XP-47H, few made it past the test stage.   (USAFM)

Above: The XP-47J was a project to evaluate the fan-cooled R-2800-61 engine. Initial plans called for an Aeroproducts counter-rotating propeller, but a standard four-blade propeller was fitted. The XP-47J program was ended in favor of the XP-72 covered below. The art on the cowling is an early rendition of Superman. (USAFM)

Right: The XP-47K was a P-47D-5-RE with a cut down rear fuselage. It was used to evaluate the installation of a bubble canopy like that used on the British Hawker Typhoon. The canopy became standard on Thunderbolts beginning with the P-47D-25-RE.
(USAFM)

Above and right: Although it did not carry a P-47 designation, the XP-72 was truly a Thunderbolt. It was powered by a P&W R-4360-13 Wasp Major 28-cylinder engine which produced 3000 horsepower. It was flown with both a standard propeller and a six-blade counter-rotating propeller. With the latter, top speed was near 500 miles-per-hour.
(Both USAFM)

P-47M

The first of three YP-47M-RE prototypes is seen here with a dorsal fin like that more commonly associated with the P-47N. Several photographs of operational P-47Ms confirm that at least a few production P-47M-1-REs were also fitted with the N-style fin strake. *(USAFM)*

Three P-47D-27-REs (42-27385. 42-27386, and 42-27388) were converted to YP-47M prototypes. These were followed by a single batch of 130 production P-47M-1-REs. This variant was designed to boost the Thunderbolt's speed to the highest possible level. To

Above: This factory fresh P-47M-1-RE has no dorsal fin, because these were not added until the aircraft arrived in England. *(USAFM)*

Left: Most P-47M-1-REs had a dorsal fin with a straight top edge from tail to fuselage. This style fin was first installed on the P-47-40-RA, and it was also retrofitted to some earlier D-models.

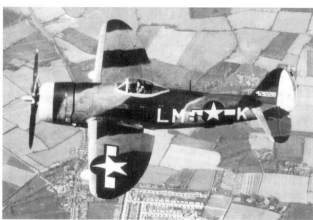

Above and right: These two views show the P-47M flown by Major Mike Quick, and it was assigned to the 62nd Fighter Squadron of the 56th Fighter Group. Codes were painted yellow. The 56th FG was the only group to fly the P-47M operationally. The Thunderbolt carries smoke generators on its wing pylons, and it was photographed from a B-17. The photo at right shows more of one of the many non-standard camouflage schemes applied by the 56th FG. Along with the aircraft's undersides, the leading edges of the wings and horizontal tails remained natural metal. *(Both USAFM)*

accomplish this, Pratt & Whitney's R-2800-14W/-57 "C-series" engine with a CH-5 turbosupercharger was fitted. In wartime emergency with water boost, this engine could develop 2800 horsepower, and the top speed climbed to nearly 475 miles-per-hour. This was a significant increase when compared to the 425 miles-per-hour of the late P-47D production blocks.

The high speed capability of the P-47M has led to reports that it was developed and used to chase down and destroy V-1 flying bombs, but by the time these aircraft arrived in England during early 1945, the threat from the V-1s had ended.

The only unit to use this variant operationally was the 56th Fighter Group at Boxted. As they were received in England, a dorsal fin was added to the spine of each aircraft. In almost all cases, this was the design with the straight upper edge as had appeared on the P-47D-40-RA. However, photographs provide evidence that at least a few P-47Ms were fitted with the fin design which was standard on the P-47N. Wing pylons were not usually installed at first, but their use became more common in a fairly short amount of time.

As they had with many of their P-47Ds, the 56th Fighter Group painted a number of unofficial and non-standard camouflage schemes on the uppersurfaces of its P-47Ms while usually leaving the undersides natural metal. Both U. S. and British colors were used including blues, grays, greens, and black. Fuselage codes were also applied in a variety of colors.

Model P-47M-1-RE
Number built 130

ENGINE . . . . P&W R-2800-57 "C-series"

PERFORMANCE
Max Speed/Altitude . . . . . . 475 mph/32,000 feet
Cruising Speed . . . . 360 mph
Normal Range/Altitude . . . 530 miles/26,000 feet
Service Ceiling . . . . 41,000 feet
Climb . . . . 13.4 minutes to 32,000 feet

WEIGHTS
Empty . . . . 10,340 pounds
Gross . . . . 15,350 pounds
Max Take off . . . . 18,250 pounds

DIMENSIONS
Span . . . . 40 feet, 9.25 inches
Wing Area . . . . 300 square feet
Length . . . . 36 feet, 1.75 inches
Height . . . . 14 feet, 8 inches

FUEL
Internal . . . . 370 gallons
External . . . . 410 gallons

P-47N

The final production variant of the Thunderbolt was the P-47N which was developed as a long range fighter. It had a larger wing and was used exclusively in the Pacific during World War II. (USAFM)

When Alexander Kartveli conceived his massive interceptor that became the XP-47B, it is unlikely that he could have imagined that it would evolve into a long range fighter with excellent fighter-bomber capabilities. But that is just what the final production variant of the Thunderbolt became.

Operations in the Pacific were usually conducted over considerable distances, and the range capability of aircraft in that theater was an important consideration. It was because of this that the P-38 Lightning had been the most successful of all USAAF fighters in the Pacific until well into 1944. Although the P-51 Mustang offered considerable range capabilities, the development of escort fighters like the P-82 Twin Mustang was begun specifically to meet the requirements found in the Pacific theater. Other studies were undertaken to extend the range capabilities of existing fighters, and in the case of the Thunderbolt, a special long range variant was produced.

P-47D-27-RE, 42-27387, was taken from production and converted to become the sole XP-47N prototype. Like the P-47M, it was fitted with the Pratt & Whitney R-2800-57 "C-series" engine and a G. E. CH-5 turbosupercharger. Evidence also indicates that the third YP-47M, 42-27388, and the XP-47K were also modified and used for this program to develop the long range P-47N.

The increase in range was accomplished through the use of a much larger wing. During testing and development, plugs of various sizes were inserted at the root of each wing to increase span, but the production aircraft had plugs that were eighteen inches in width. The elliptical wing design, common to all previous Thunderbolts,

was altered. Trailing edge taper at the ailerons was decreased, and the tips were blunt. This resulted in an additional twenty-two square feet of wing area as compared to earlier variants. The landing gear was modified, and because of the plugs, it was further out on the wing than on other variants. This increased the wheel tread to 18 feet, 5 13/16 inches.

Longer ranges required more fuel, and the internal fuel capacity was increased from the 370 gallons in the P-47D to 570 gallons in the P-47N. The extra two hundred gallons were carried in interconnected fuel tanks mounted in the enlarged inboard section of each wing. Up to 620 gallons of external fuel could also be carried in two 310-gallon drop tanks, but a speed limitation of 200 miles-per-hour was imposed when these large tanks were in place. A more common external fuel load consisted of a combination of two 165-gallon wing tanks and a 110-gallon belly tank. But it was possible for a P-47N to take off with 1170 gallons of fuel and a gross weight exceeding 20,000 pounds. With this load, the aircraft could fly for over twelve hours and have a radius of action in excess of 1,300 miles. To relieve pilot fatigue on flights of such duration, arm rests were installed on the seat beginning with the P-47N-15-RE.

Although not originally installed on the P-47N-1-RE, stubs for 5-inch rockets became standard on the P-47N-5-RE. P-47N-1-REs, which were retrofitted with the rocket capability in the field, were redesignated P-47N-2-REs. A combination of these rockets and up to 3,000 pounds of bombs made the P-47N an impressive fighter-bomber as

The larger wing is clearly evident in this flying view. Stubs were added at the root of the wing, and this caused the inner landing gear doors to be away from the fuselage rather than next to it, as was the case on other Thunderbolts. The outer panels of the wings were less tapered, and the wing tips were blunt. (USAFM)

Several different antenna arrangements were used on the spine of P-47Ns, and this post-war P-47N seems to have all of them. Two antenna masts straddle the dorsal fin, while another is just aft of the open canopy. A loop antenna is between it and the fin. The Curtiss Electric symmetrical paddleblade propeller seems to be the one used almost exclusively on the P-47N. (USAFM)

P-47Ns were still in service when the U. S. Army Air Forces became the U. S. Air Force in 1947, and they were redesignated as F-47Ns at that time. Note the red bar in the national insignia, and that the insignia is located completely aft of the intercooler doors. A buzz number is painted on the side of the fuselage. Some of the post-war F-47Ns were relegated to training roles and were redesignated TF-47Ns.
(USAFM)

well as the long range escort fighter it was intended to be.

In spite of the increased weight, the P-47N was second only to the P-47M as the fastest of all production variants. It could attain a top speed of 467 miles-per-hour at 32,000 feet, and its service ceiling was 40,000 feet where it still exceeded 435 miles-per-hour.

Production was divided into seven blocks not counting the P-47N-2-RE modification in the field. There were 550 P-47N-1-REs built as well as a like number of P-47N-5-REs. The latter was produced with the rocket stubs, and they also had the AN/APS-13 tail warning radar.

The next production block was the P-47N-15-RE, and as stated earlier, it had arm rests on the seat to reduce pilot fatigue. A K-14A or -14B gun sight replaced the standard K-14, and other relatively minor detail changes were also made to the two hundred aircraft in this production block.

The Evansville plant built 149 P-47N-20-RAs, while 200 P-47N-20-REs were produced at Farmingdale. An emergency fuel system was added, changes were made to the radio equipment, and other minor detail modifications and improvements were made to these aircraft.

The final two hundred Thunderbolts were in the P-47N-25-RE production block. Again there were detail improvements to equipment, but there was one external change that was noticeable to the eye. The navigation lights on the wing tips were deleted from the leading edge of the tip and replaced with smaller units at the center of the tip's outer edge. The last P-47N-25-RE was completed in October 1945 and delivered to the USAAF in December, thus ending the largest production run for any U. S. built fighter aircraft in history. The total of all vari-

ants had reached 15,683 Thunderbolts.

All P-47Ns that served in combat during World War II were used in the Pacific and operated from the island of Ie Shima. The 318th, 413th, 414th, and 507th Fighter Groups all flew the N-model during the final months in the war against Japan.

P-47Ns were retained in post-war service with the U. S. Army Air Forces and then with the U. S. Air Force and Air National Guard. In 1947, when the U. S. Air Force was established as a separate service, the "P" designation for pursuit was dropped in favor of an "F" for fighter. All Thunderbolts became F-47s at that time. In their later service, some F-47Ns were relegated exclusively to training duties and were called TF-47Ns.

The 14th, 21st, 56th, and 332nd Fighter Groups all operated P-47Ns after World War II in the regular Army Air Forces and the U. S. Air Force. The last Thunderbolts in regular Air Force service were retired in October 1949 by the 14th Fighter Group. Others continued to serve with various Air National Guard squadrons.

Model P-47N
Number built 1,816

Data below for: P-47N-1-RE

ENGINE . . . . P&W R-2800-57 "C-series"

PERFORMANCE
Max Speed/Altitude . . . . . . 467 mph/32,000 feet
Cruising Speed . . . . 300 mph
Max Range/Altitude . . . . 2,200 miles/25,000 feet
Normal Range/Altitude . . . 800 miles/25,000 feet
Service Ceiling . . . . 40,000 feet
Climb . . . . 14.2 minutes to 25,000 feet

WEIGHTS
Empty . . . . 10,988 pounds
Gross . . . . 13,823 pounds
Max Take off . . . . 21,200 pounds

DIMENSIONS
Span . . . . 42 feet, 6.8 inches
Wing Area . . . . 322 square feet
Length . . . . 36 feet, 1.75 inches
Height . . . . 14 feet, 6 inches

FUEL
Internal . . . . 556 gallons
External . . . . 700 gallons

Many F-47Ns spent most of their operational service in the Air National Guard. Lt. Col. Ollie O. Simpson flew this F-47N-25-RE when he commanded the 128th Fighter Squadron of the Georgia Air National Guard. The flash on the cowl and fuselage side is dark blue. *(USAFM)*

P-47N COCKPIT DETAILS

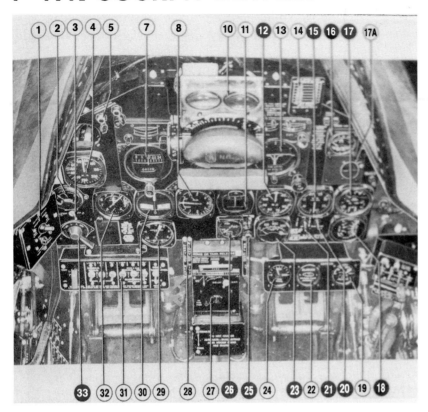

1. Propeller Switch Box
2. Ammeter
3. Battery Switch
4. Airspeed Indicator
5. Landing Gear Warning Light
6. (Deleted)
7. Directional Gyro Indicator
8. Rate of Climb Indicator
9. (Deleted)
10. K-14B Gunsight
11. Compass
12. Manifold Pressure Gage
13. Gyro Horizon Indicator
14. Diving Speed Limitation Chart
15. Engine Tachometer
16. Carburetor Air Temperature Gage
17. Engine Gage Unit
17A. Radio Compass Indicator
18. Fuel Quantity Gage
19. Oxygen Pressure Gage
20. Starter Switch
21. Engine Primer Switch
22. Oxygen Flow Indicator
23. Cylinder Head Temperature Gage
24. Hydraulic Pressure Gage
25. Fuel Level Warning Light
26. Water Pressure Gage
27. Rocket Selector Panel
28. Mechanical Bomb or Tank Release
29. Accelerometer
30. Band and Turn Indicator
31. Armament Selector Panel
32. Altimeter
33. Ignition Switch

The photographs on page 45 show the cockpit of a P-47N-25-RE after it had served with the Air National Guard. The three photos on this page were taken from the operations manual for the P-47N, and they reflect what the cockpit looked like during World War II. Keys for the instrument panel can be found at right. (USAFM)

Details on the left side of the cockpit are indicated here. Keys are provided below. (USAFM)

The right side of the cockpit is shown in this view. Again, keys for the features are given below. (USAFM)

1. Gunsight Selector-Dimmer
2. Hydraulic Hand Pump
3. Trim Tab Control Unit
4. Wing Flap Control
5. Main Switch Panel
6. Landing Gear Control Handle
7. Landing Gear Control Safety Latch
8. Fuel Selector Valves
9. Engine Control Quadrant
10. Circuit Protector Panel
11. Canopy Control Switch
12. Propeller Switch Box

1. Defroster Control
2. Recognition Lights Switch Box
3. Cockpit Vent Control
4. AN/ARC-3 Controls
5. Oxygen Demand Regulator
6. AN/ARN-7 Radio Controls
7. SCR-695A Radio Controls
8. BC-453B or E Radio Controls
9. Secret Radio Detonator
10. Cockpit Swivel Light

P-47N ROCKET INSTALLATION

Above: Although being intended as a long range escort fighter, the P-47N could carry a considerable amount of external stores.   (Graser collection)

Left: This close-up provides a look at the rockets and bomb under the right wing.   (USAFM)

Below left and right: A triple rocket launcher was designed to fit on the pylon as shown at left. By combining this with the five sets of stubs under each wing, a total of sixteen 5-inch rockets could be carried.
*   (Both USAFM)*

P-47N DETAIL DIFFERENCES

The P-47N had blunt wing tips as compared to the curved tips on other variants. On most N-models, the navigation lights were on the leading edge of the tip as they were on other Thunderbolts. But on the P-47N-25-RE, the navigation lights were mounted at the center of the tip as shown here. Also note the three identification lights under the right wing tip.

The light on the left wing tip is shown here. The retractable landing/taxi light is also visible under the wing.

On all previous versions of the Thunderbolt, the inner main gear doors were mounted right next to the fuselage. But with the addition of the plugs at the root of each wing, the inner doors on the P-47N were further out from the fuselage as illustrated in this front view.

Compare this main gear wheel to that shown on page 30. The design is different, and most noticeably, there are eight spokes instead of only six.

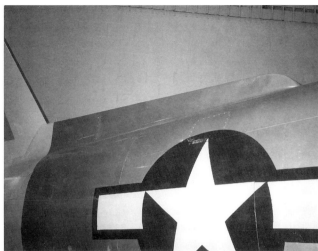

Above and right: The P-47N had a larger dorsal fin than that seen on late P-47Ds and most P-47Ms. Its design is visible in these two views. However, it should be noted that photos indicate that this fin was also fitted to some P-47Ms.

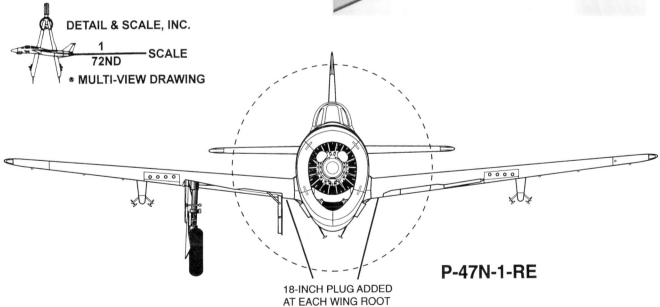

DETAIL & SCALE, INC.

$\frac{1}{72\text{ND}}$ SCALE

® MULTI-VIEW DRAWING

P-47N-1-RE

18-INCH PLUG ADDED
AT EACH WING ROOT

DETAIL & SCALE 1/72nd SCALE COPYRIGHT © DRAWINGS BY LLOYD S. JONES

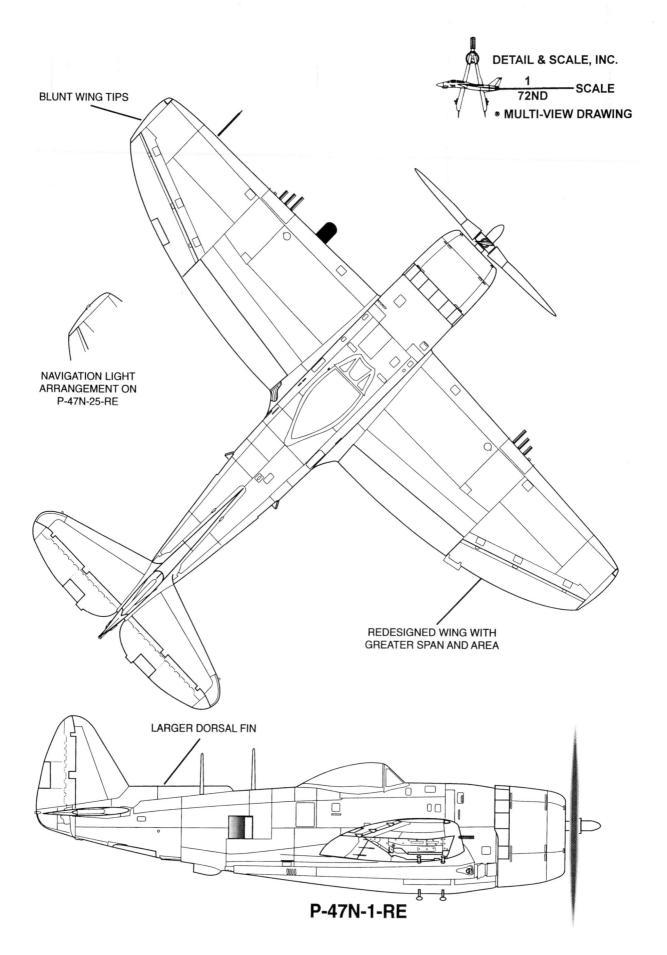

BLUNT WING TIPS

NAVIGATION LIGHT
ARRANGEMENT ON
P-47N-25-RE

REDESIGNED WING WITH
GREATER SPAN AND AREA

LARGER DORSAL FIN

P-47N-1-RE

DETAIL & SCALE 1/72nd SCALE COPYRIGHT © DRAWINGS BY LLOYD S. JONES

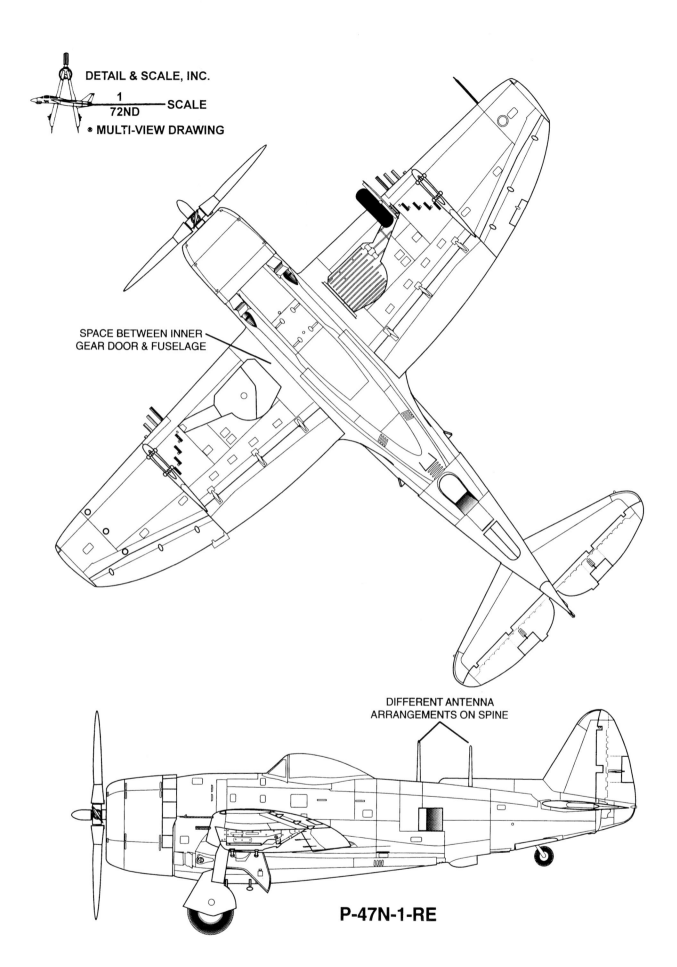

SPACE BETWEEN INNER
GEAR DOOR & FUSELAGE

DIFFERENT ANTENNA
ARRANGEMENTS ON SPINE

P-47N-1-RE

DETAIL & SCALE 1/72nd SCALE COPYRIGHT © DRAWINGS BY LLOYD S. JONES

MODELERS SECTION

Note: There have been numerous plastic model kits of the P-47 Thunderbolt released since the 1950s. Due to space limitations, complete reviews are included for only the best kits in each scale. Review summaries are provided for older kits that have more value to collectors than to serious scale modelers.

1/144th SCALE KITS

Academy/Minicraft P-47D Bubbletop Thunderbolt

Numerous shape and outline problems prevent this little kit from being built as an accurate model of the P-47. At the front, the propeller does not represent any of the four used on Thunderbolts, although it could be re-worked into a fairly good Curtiss Electric asymmetrical paddleblade propeller with some filing or sanding. The instructions show a three-blade propeller, and it appears that this kit may once have been issued with a propeller with only three blades. There is no representation of the engine in the cowling, and the cowl itself is not the correct shape. The keel is way too deep, and this distorts the shape of the lower fuselage.

Each main landing gear is molded as one piece and is a satisfactory representation of the real thing considering the small scale of the kit. However, the main gear wells are relatively shallow indentions in the underside of the wings, and they look unrealistic. An option is provided to build this kit with the landing gear closed as well as in the extended position.

There are two pylons to go under the wings, but each has a large slot. Neither the bombs nor the fuel tanks that come in the kit fit into these slots very well, so some filling and sanding is required to make the pylons and stores look right.

The canopy is a single clear piece that fits on top of the fuselage. There is absolutely no representation of the cockpit interior, nor is there even a hole in the fuselage where the cockpit should be. Surface detailing is lacking, and it isn't very accurate. The shroud for the turbosupercharger is too large and is positioned too far forward.

The guns and the pitot probe are molded on the wings and are acceptable for this small scale. But the antenna mast is split vertically on the fuselage halves, and when the fuselage is assembled, it looks too thick. It would be better to cut off the part on the left fuselage and use only the half on the right fuselage.

Overall, this is not one of the better 1/144th scale kits on the market, and we recommend the Crown/Revell release as the better choice in this scale.

Crown/Revell P-47D Bubbletop Thunderbolt

This is clearly the better of the two plastic kits of the Thunderbolt in 1/144th scale. The shape and outline of the kit is quite good and surface detailing is better than that on the Academy/Minicraft model. A trim tab is represented on the right aileron, and it should not be there. Otherwise, the representation of the control surfaces is well done for a kit this size.

Originally issued by Crown, this model once had a three-blade propeller as shown in the photograph. Our sample of the Revell issue has a correct four-blade propeller that is a good reproduction of the Curtiss Electric symmetrical design.

There is fair representation of engine cylinders and the gear reduction casing inside the cowling. The cowl flaps are likewise nicely represented. The guns are molded on the wings, but there is no pitot probe. This can easily be added using some stretched plastic sprue. The antenna mast on the fuselage is also missing and will have to be made from scratch.

Each main landing gear is one piece, and the wheels have spokes indicating that the cover is not present. These are adequate, but could be improved. This is one place where the Academy/Minicraft kit is better.

The pylons are molded as part of the wings, and they look much better than those in the Academy/Minicraft kit. But the two bombs are very crude. Using the bombs or fuel tanks from the Academy/Minicraft kit would be a better choice, or the pylons could simply be left empty. However, the drop tank for the centerline station in this Crown/Revell model is quite good.

There is no cockpit interior, and one should be added with some scrap parts. Simply adding some basics, like an instrument panel, seat, pilot's armor, and control column, would go a long way toward improving the appearance of the model. The canopy is a single clear part that needs a little filing along the rails in order for it to fit flush on top of the fuselage.

There are some sink marks that have to be filled, and a bit of filling and sanding is needed where the wings and the horizontal tails join the fuselage. But with a little work, this kit can end up being a nice little model of a bubbletop Thunderbolt.

Paul Gold contributed to the reviews of the 1/144th scale kits.

Paul Gold used the Academy/Minicraft 1/144th scale P-47D to build this model. The kit has several very noticeable inaccuracies, and detailing is lacking even for such a small scale. *(Gold)*

The Crown/Revell P-47D is the better of the two available 1/144th scale Thunderbolts. *(Gold)*

1/94th SCALE KIT

Aurora P-47D Bubbletop Thunderbolt

Issued in 1963 with a retail price of thirty-nine cents, this gear-up "flying" model came with a two-piece stand and no landing gear. Instead, the gear doors were scribed into the underside of the wings and fuselage in the retracted position.

More typical of kits from the 1950s, this model had the decal locations etched into the plastic along with the surface detailing. Neither was very accurate. Likewise, the outline of most parts is inaccurate, and the best that can be said is that the finished model "resembles" a Thunderbolt.

This kit might have some interest to collectors, but it is not one that a modeler would want to use to build an accurate model of the P-47.

1/72nd SCALE KITS

Academy P-47D Razorback and Bubbletop Thunderbolts

At press time for this book, Academy had announced both razorback and bubbletop Thunderbolts in 1/72nd scale. A specific release date had not been set, but it appeared that these kits would be available by mid-1998. Considering the fact that none of the 1/72nd scale Thunderbolt models presently on the market are truly excellent, these kits could become very welcome additions to the Academy line.

Airfix/MPC P-47D Razorback Thunderbolt

One of the earlier models of the Thunderbolt in 1/72nd scale, this kit has most of the major shapes correct. Surface scribing is in the form of raised rivets and engraved lines to show the control surfaces. One error is that there is an adjustable trim tab on the right aileron, but this was not on the real aircraft.

Four clear parts are provided, and these include the windscreen, framed canopy, bulletproof glass, and the landing light under the left wing.

The engine is a separate part rather than being molded inside the cowling. It isn't great, but it will satisfy many modelers who do not wish to find an after-market engine. A nice Hamilton-Standard propeller is provided, but the blades need to be thinned a little. It

The author used the old Airfix kit in 1/72nd scale to build this model of Lt. Col. Neal Kearby's "Firey Ginger."

should be noted that many razorback Thunderbolts used the original Curtiss Electric propeller.

This kit is now over thirty years old, and kits from the early 1960s usually lacked detailing. Except for the engine, this Thunderbolt model is no exception. A pilot figure is included for the cockpit, and the main gear wells are open. The landing gear itself is oversimplified, and the main gear wheels leave a lot to be desired.

With a basically correct shape, this kit could be the basis of a nice model of the Thunderbolt if the modeler wanted to do the detailing that Airfix left off. But with better kits of the P-47D razorbacks available, this one is best left to the collectors.

Frog P-47D Razorback Thunderbolt

Perhaps the first of all of the 1/72nd scale Thunderbolts, this Frog kit shows its age. Decal locations are engraved into the plastic, there is almost no detailing, and there are a number of shape and outline problems. It features bombs for the wing pylons, and a centerline tank is provided to go under the fuselage. The propeller looks like the original thin Curtiss Electric design, and it may still be the best 1/72nd scale representation of this propeller that is available. But all things considered, this old model only has value to collectors.

Fujimi P-47D Razorback Thunderbolt

Another one of the older 1/72nd scale Thunderbolt kits, this model is no longer generally available. It is quite crude by today's standards, and it is plagued by numerous inaccuracies and a lack of detailing.

Like the other early Thunderbolt kits, this one cannot be recommended to the serious modeler.

Hasegawa P-47D Razorback & Bubbletop Thunderbolts

Although it cannot be considered an excellent kit, the Hasegawa Thunderbolt is presently one of the two better P-47 models available in 1/72nd scale. It has been issued in both razorback and bubbletop configurations, with the only differences being the fuselage halves and canopies. There is also a small part representing the head rest and the top of the pilot's armor in the bubbletop version. Otherwise, the kits are the same, and the following comments apply to both.

The propeller included is the original Curtiss Electric design with the thin blades, but it isn't very accurate. A replacement needs to be made from scratch for any of the Curtiss Electric props, but a decent Hamilton-Standard propeller can be obtained from the Airfix or Jo Han models. Although the engine is better than found in some 1/72nd scale Thunderbolt kits, it lacks the obvious magneto covers on the crankcase. An after-market R-2800 engine will look much better than what comes in the kit. The two dividers in the intake ducting below the engine are missing.

There is also very little detailing inside the cockpit. This is easily fixed with a cockpit specifically designed for this model from True Details. Unfortunately, there is no after-market help for the open main gear wells, and the modeler is left to fill and detail these with plastic card and other parts. The struts are too long, and the cover plates on the wheels are incorrect. Each cover should be simply a flat disc. True Details makes a set of P-47 wheels in

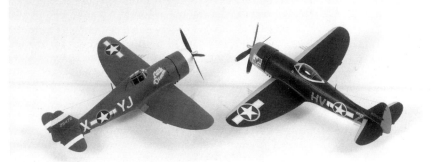

Hasegawa makes both razorback and bubbletop P-47Ds in 1/72nd scale. J. C. Bahr built one of each for the review in this book, but he modified the bubbletop to P-47M standards. (Liles)

1/72nd scale, and we suggest using these instead.

We have read reviews that have stated that the fuselage is about a scale foot too long. However, this does not check out with the measurements we have or the drawings we developed. This may be because the reviewer used a well known set of drawings published elsewhere that are too short and which have other errors with respect to where items are located on the fuselage.

Surface scribing is recessed, and for the most part it is nicely done. However, the leading edge of each elevator is a little too far aft. It is not so bad as to be easily noticed, and rescribing it would probably be more work than it is worth. The shape of the trailing edge of the elevators is a little off, but again, it is not worth worrying about.

The wings are good except for the fact that the guns are mounted in line with the leading edge rather than being parallel to the ground. This is a problem with all P-47 kits in 1/72nd scale, and it needs to be corrected.

The canopy and windscreen in the razorback kits are usable as they are, but the vacu-formed ones from Squadron are better and can be displayed in the open position. But note in our drawings that the sliding framed canopy did have a bit of a "bubble" to it when viewed from the side. This is evident in some photos, and it is certainly obvious when you study a real aircraft. The bubble canopy is another story. The two forward pieces of the framework are parallel, and they should not be. This makes the front piece of glass too narrow at the base. There are no other clear parts, so the modeler is left to paint the navigation lights on the wing tips, the landing light under the left wing, and the identification lights under the right wing tip. As an alternative, these can be made from clear scrap plastic.

There is a choice of 500-pound bombs or 108-gallon drop tanks to go on the wing pylons. Unfortunately, there is no representation of the fuel lines or shackle that should be on the fuselage station. It would take a little work to add these, but it would be well worth the effort. It also offers the possibility of adding a centerline store.

While this may be one of the two better Thunderbolt kits in 1/72nd scale, it leaves a lot to be desired. An after-market engine and cockpit interior will be needed, and the canopy and propeller must be replaced with parts from other kits or made from scratch. Most modelers will also want to use the main gear wheels from True Details.

J. C. Bahr and Norris Graser contributed to this review.

Heller P-47N Thunderbolt

Although this is the only 1/72nd scale kit of the P-47N that has been issued in quantity, it is so inaccurate that it would be simpler to convert a P-47D bubbletop kit to a P-47N than to correct all the problems with this one.

The most important difference between the P-47N and previous Thunderbolts was the larger wing with increased span and area. But the Heller wing is completely unusable. It is flat on top and curved underneath rather than the other way around, as it should be. The landing gear is positioned too close to the fuselage instead of being moved outward as it was on the real P-47N. The landing gear itself is also inaccurate, and the pylons are located too far outboard.

There are minor problems too. The deflector between the oil cooler door and waste gate is represented as another door with a vent behind it. The bombs are not very good, and the rockets are even worse. The launch stubs are in the wrong places under the wings and the hinges for the flaps and ailerons are also inaccurate.

The engine is the wrong version, having the bullet-shaped crankcase rather than the cylindrical one. The propeller attempts to represent the Curtiss Electric symmetrical design but falls short.

Almost anywhere you look on this model, there are glaring problems and inaccuracies. The cowling is too big and too low, the tail is too small. Any modeler who really wants to build a P-47N in 1/72nd scale would be better

This Heller 1/72nd scale kit of the P-47N has a lot of inaccuracies that are difficult to correct. Jeff Zimmerman built this model of an aircraft from the 403rd Fighter Squadron of the 507th Fighter Group. (Dyckes)

off trying to find the High Planes limited run kit which is reviewed next.

High Planes Models P-47N Thunderbolt

This is a limited run injection molded kit from Australia. It may be difficult to find, but for anyone wanting to build a 1/72nd scale model of the P-47N, the search will be well worth the effort. The only alternative is the Heller kit which is so inaccurate that it cannot be considered.

For a limited run model, this kit has excellent recessed panel lines and surface detail. But fit and detailing are not as good. The eight machine guns must be provided by the modeler, and the holes to locate them in the wings must be drilled out. During construction, parts must always be test fitted, and the modeler must be prepared to remove plastic with a knife or use a file to get parts to fit together properly. The instructions even warn about this necessity. But the instructions are also simplistic and incomplete by most standards, so this further amplifies the need for test fitting of each step by the modeler as he proceeds. The instructions show the pitot probe on the right wing, but it should be on the left.

Although most parts are plastic, the landing gear struts are white metal and the wheels are resin. The hole where each strut joins the wing must be drilled out. The canopy is vacu-formed, and with careful trimming, it fits nicely on the fuselage.

The interior has only the basics, and adding some details, particularly on the cockpit sides, will help. Using parts from the True Details P-47D through M cockpit set may be the simplest route although the details are not exactly right for a P-47N. In 1/72nd scale, the differences probably would not be noticeable.

Although it takes some extra work to get all the parts together, what makes this kit so valuable is that it is much more accurate than the Heller P-47N. While not perfect, it doesn't have the noticeable flaws of the Heller model.

Review sample courtesy of Precision Enterprises Unltd.

Jo Han P-47D Bubbletop and Razorback Thunderbolt

Right out of the box, this is our pick as the best

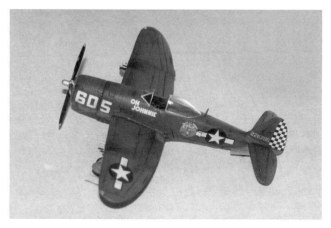

The Jo Han P-47D can be built as a razorback or a bubbletop. The author chose the bubbletop option to build this model of Ray Knight's aircraft, "Oh Johnnie."

Thunderbolt model in 1/72nd scale. It is not without its faults, but there are less of them than on any other kit in this scale.

Either a bubbletop or a razorback P-47D can be built from this kit, but fitting the spine on the fuselage halves will require a bit of filling and sanding. The panel lines are engraved, and while this is a desirable feature, rescribing the line between the fuselage halves and the spine is a little difficult with all that filling. An adjustable trim tab is scribed into the right aileron, but it should not be there. Only the left aileron had an adjustable trim tab, while the right aileron had a fixed balance tab. The fixed tab is accurately represented in the kit. The shape of the forward fuselage is slightly tapered when viewed from the side, and this is incorrect. Otherwise, shape and outlines are very good.

A Hamilton-Standard propeller is supplied in the kit, and it is pretty good. A little thinning of the blades will help. The oiling bosses, which are located on the hub between the blades, are missing, but they could easily be added using stretched sprue. The engine is adequate, but the dividers in the intake below it are missing.

The landing gear is much better than that found in the Hasegawa kit, but the main gear wells still need to be closed in with plastic card. There is no well for the tail wheel at all. Some extra detailing will also add to the appearance of the wheels. Again, a better alternative is to use the True Details set of Thunderbolt wheels.

The locating holes for the pylons are slightly too far outboard, but it is fairly simple to reposition them since they are separate pieces. Unfortunately, there is no representation of the fuselage station. As with all 1/72nd scale Thunderbolts, the guns need to be repositioned so that they are parallel to the ground. We also added a pitot probe made from stretched sprue.

The canopy is the best in any 1/72nd scale Thunderbolt kit, but it and the windscreen are the only two clear parts. The modeler must paint the navigation lights on the tips of the wings as well as the landing light under the left wing. We also drilled out and painted the three identification lights under the right wing.

The cockpit lacks detailing, but we found that with only minimal trimming, the True Details cockpit fits nicely into this model.

As with the Hasegawa kit, this model takes some extra work and detailing in order to become a quality model.

Matchbox P-47D Razorback Thunderbolt

This kit has some good points, but overall, it simply does not measure up to the Jo Han and Hasegawa models. The propeller is a fair representation of a Curtiss Electric paddleblade which can be used after some thinning and slight reshaping of the blades. See the drawings and photographs in this book for the correct blade shape.

The shape of the cowling looks correct, and this is always a point of interest, because it is one of the defining features of the Thunderbolt. However, the cowl flaps are not represented as well as they should be, and for most P-47Ds, the lower two should be reduced in width as illustrated in the drawings in this book. The scoop in the lower cowl needs to be removed and replaced with one made from scratch that has the dividers in the ducting. The best that can be said about the engine is that it is adequate, but the noticeable magneto covers should be added from scratch. Most modelers will want to replace it with an after-market engine or at least a better one from another kit.

The main gear wheels are a plus, being the only ones to represent the wheels without the covers so that the spokes are visible. Some tread should be added to the tires, but otherwise they are the best in any 1/72nd scale kit of the P-47.

There are some shape problems with the fuselage, particularly on the underside. Surface detailing leaves a lot to be desired as one might expect from a Matchbox kit. It is both incomplete and inaccurate in places. Even the shell chutes under the wings are missing. As much as for any other reason, it is because of this poor surface detailing that we cannot recommend this kit.

Norris Graser contributed to this review.

MPM XP-47H Thunderbolt

For modelers who would like to try something a little different from the usual P-47D, M, and N Thunderbolt models, MPM of Czechoslovakia has this kit of the XP-47H in 1/72nd scale. Its molding is rough, being typical for a limited run kit, but the basic shapes are there, and a competent modeler can build a nice model from it if care is taken during assembly. There are no line-up pins or holes, so the modeler must be careful to make sure parts are in the proper position before the glue sets.

Many parts have some flash that needs to be cleaned up, and each is attached firmly to the sprue tree. Plastic stubs are on many of the larger parts, and these too must be removed before construction begins. Carefully cut the parts from the tree using clippers. Trying to break them off will inevitably damage the parts. The canopy is vacu-formed, but all other parts are molded in light gray plastic. Surface detailing is in the form of recessed lines which are generally well done and reasonably accurate. Even the balance tabs are represented on the right aileron and the two elevators, and the actuators for all trim tabs are present. But the ones for the trim tabs on the elevators should be on the lower surfaces, not on top as shown on the instruction sheet. Simply reversing the horizontal tails will correct this problem.

The cockpit has only a seat, floor, control column, instrument panel, and rear bulkhead. A decal is included for the instrument panel, but other detailing is required. The sides would be similar to those in a P-47D-15-RA.

The XP-47H originally had oval-shaped holes on each side of the spine. These were later covered with air scoops to increase the flow of cooling air. But the kit provides only one scoop, and the instructions show it going on the right side. The simplest solution is to leave it off and build the plane as it appeared when it began test flights. But if the scoops are desired, a second one will have to be made from scratch. The large air scoop beneath the fuselage has an interior with the air flow dividers to avoid a hollow look.

The landing gear is rough, and each main gear wheel and tire is split vertically. It would be better to use landing gear struts, doors, and a tail wheel from another

1/72nd scale kit, and the True Details wheels are the best choice for the main gear.

While this is not a state-of-the-art kit, it does offer an alternative to the common Thunderbolt variants. With a little work it can be a nice addition to any collection.

Lindberg P-47B Thunderbolt

The box art states that this is a P-47B, but features in the kit indicate an early P-47D. This very early plastic model is not really a scale rendition of the real thing, but it is more of an approximate representation. As such, any value it may have is only with collectors.

Revell P-47D Bubbletop Thunderbolt

Dating back over thirty years, this was one of the first 1/72nd scale kits of the P-47D to have the bubble canopy. Although its overall shape is not too bad, it is oversimplified and lacks details. There are also many inaccuracies in what detailing is provided, and the surfaces are covered with rivets that must be removed. We cannot recommend this kit as one to build.

Over twenty-five years ago, the author used the Revell 1/72nd scale P-47D to build this model of Lt. Col. Francis Gabreski's famous Thunderbolt.

1/48th SCALE KITS

Academy/Minicraft P-47N

Molded in light gray plastic, this kit has the rocket stubs under the wings indicating a P-47N-5-RE or later. It could also be used to represent a P-47N-2-RE, which was a P-47N-1-RE with the rocket stubs added in the field. Although the panel lines are recessed, individual access panels stand proud of the surrounding area. While this is not too severe, it is not the best representation of the aircraft's skin.

A wide variety of external stores is provided including three different sizes of fuel tanks, ten rockets, and both 500 and 1000-pound bombs. Save the triple-tube rocket launchers for another kit, because the P-47N used the 5-inch rockets on the zero-length stubs.

The opening for the cockpit is incorrect in that the area behind the instrument panel is open. This causes the back of the instrument panel to be visible through the windscreen. The cockpit can be improved with the True Details cockpit set designed specifically for this kit.

The engine is wrong for a P-47N, because it does not have the cylindrical crankcase with the dozens of exposed

Jim Roeder used the Minicraft 1/48th scale P-47N to build this model of "Expected Goose." Both gun bays can be built in the open position on this model. (Roeder)

bolts that characterized the R-2800-57 used in the P-47M and P-47N. Correct aftermarket engines are available from Aeromaster and Teknics. The propeller represents the Curtiss Electric asymmetrical paddleblade design, but most P-47Ns had the symmetrical design.

Both weighted and unweighted tires are included in the kit, but the weighted ones are too flat. Use the unweighted ones, and if desired, file a smaller flat place on them. Another option is provided in the form of intercooler doors that can be built open or closed.

Panels for both gun bays are separate pieces that can be shown in the open position revealing the guns and their ammunition chutes. The blast tubes are correctly aligned in the leading edge of the wings.

The clear parts are very good and include the windscreen, canopy, wing tip lights, retractable landing/taxi light, and three identification lights under the right wing.

With after-market help for the cockpit and engine, this model can be completed as a nice replica of the P-47N, and we give it the nod as being slightly better overall than the ProModeler kit.

Jim Roeder contributed to this review.

Academy P-47D Bubbletop Thunderbolt

Released in December 1997, this kit shares a lot in common with the older Academy/Minicraft P-47N covered immediately above. In fact, three of the five sprue trees containing the light gray parts are identical. New parts include the wings, fuselage halves, a 150-gallon flat fuel tank, Curtiss Electric symmetrical propeller, and the landing gear. The wheels do not have the covers, but they do have the correct number of spokes. This is important, because the number of spokes was six on the P-47D and eight on the P-47N. However, the wheels for the P-47N remain in this kit as well, so be sure to use the correct ones for the P-47D when building this model.

Like the P-47N kit, this model also has the slightly raised access panels on the aircraft's skin, and both gun bays can be built in the open position to display the guns and their ammunition feed chutes. The extensive selection of external stores is also the same for both kits.

The cockpit has the corrugated floor, indicating that this model is best used to build a P-47D-25-RE through a P-47D-28-RE. Likewise, there are no compressibility flaps under the wings, and this also indicates a P-47D-28-RE or earlier bubbletop Thunderbolt. The cockpit detailing is fair, but it could stand some improvement. With some trimming, the KMC cockpit set could be used for aircraft up through the P-47-28-RE block. Building this model as an aircraft from the -30 or -40 production block would require a different cockpit floor, the addition of compressibility flaps, and possibly a dorsal fin depending on the specific aircraft being modeled.

Clear parts are of good quality, and they are provided for the windscreen, canopy, wing tip lights, retractable landing light, the three identification lights under the right wing, and the glass in the gun sight.

Except for the raised access panels, the surface detail is good, and it is accurate for the most part. Academy is one of the few manufacturers to get the aileron trim tabs right by leaving the adjustable tab off of the right aileron. The fixed balance tab is present on the right aileron as it should be, and each elevator also has the correct balance tab. The drain cocks, which are located just aft of the wing root on the right side of the fuselage, are missing, but otherwise the surface detailing looks very good except for those raised access panels.

A seam line will be inside each main wheel well when the parts are joined, and it is a little tricky to get rid of. Doing so will almost surely remove some of the ribs on the upper surface of the wells.

This is a very good model, and it ranks with the Hasegawa kits and the Monogram razorback P-47D as the best Thunderbolts in 1/48th scale.

Hasegawa P-47D Bubbletop Thunderbolt

This kit has been released as a P-47D-25-RE, and also as a P-47D-30 or 40-RE. The only difference between the two versions is that the latter has two etched metal parts to represent the compressibility flaps under the wings. These two parts are simply to be glued down on to the

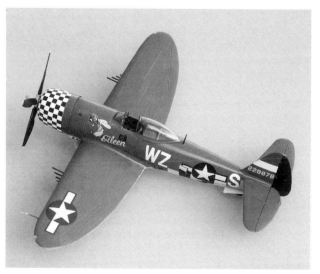

The best Thunderbolt kit in 1/48th scale is from Hasegawa. It was used by Stan Parker to build this model of "Eileen" from the 84th Fighter Squadron of the 78th Fighter Group. (Parker)

plastic wing, and there are no guides to indicate exactly where they are to be located. Both the -28 and -30/-40 issues have the dorsal fin as used on the -40, but it is in the form of two separate parts. The instructions only refer to them for the appropriate variant.

These kits are clearly the best of any Thunderbolt models issued to date. Problems are relatively minor and include the engine which appears to be copied from Hasegawa's Hellcat model. To correct this, move the distributor even with the two magnetos and use some sandpaper to give the nose of the crankcase more of a bullet shape by increasing its taper to the front.

The other area that needs help is the cockpit. For the P-47D-28-RA, we recommend using the KMC (Kendall) cockpit set that provides a greater degree of detailing. But modelers should note that Thunderbolts up through the P-47D-28-RA had corrugated floors as provided in the kit and by KMC. Beginning with the P-47D-30-RE and RA, the floor was flat. Evidence of this is provided in the photographs of the P-47D-30-RE on pages 40 and 41. Hasegawa failed to take this into account when they reissued the kit as a -30/-40. For these later P-47D production blocks, we recommend True Details cockpit set 48466 which is for a P-47D-30/-40-RE. It has the correct flat floor as well as other changes in details.

Both Curtiss Electric symmetrical and asymmetrical propellers are included, but if a Hamilton-Standard prop is desired, KMC comes to the rescue again with one made of resin. KMC also offers both of the Curtiss Electric paddleblade propellers as well. We also recommend the separate control surfaces KMC makes for this model. By dropping the flaps and repositioning the other control surfaces, a good model can be made even better.

Fit is excellent except that a small amount of filling may be needed where the trailing edge of the wing assembly joins the lower fuselage. Otherwise, the kit can be built without the use of any modeling putty.

The guns are mounted parallel to the ground as they should be, and other detailing is likewise well executed and correct for the most part. One exception is that Hasegawa put adjustable trim tabs on both ailerons, and this is wrong. There should only be one on the left aileron, and the right aileron should have a fixed balance tab. This feature is missing from the kit. Also, the very noticeable drain cocks on the right side of the fuselage near the trailing edge of the wing root are not represented.

The ducting in the intake at the bottom of the cowling is correct, and even the fronts of the radiators are provided. Surface detailing is recessed, accurate, and well defined. If the pylons are left off, strakes are visible under the wings, and this is as it was on the real aircraft.

Clear parts are excellent and are even included for the three identification lights under the right wing. Be sure to paint the inside of each of these the appropriate color before gluing them in place.

At press time for this book, Hasegawa had released only the bubbletop variants mentioned at the beginning of this review. But an announcement had also been made for the future release of razorback versions. Undoubtedly, any such release will be the same as these kits, except that they will have new fuselage and canopy parts.

Norris Graser and Jim Roeder contributed to this review.

Hawk, Testors, Italeri P-47D Thunderbolt

Originally released by Hawk over thirty years ago, this kit has parts to build a razorback or bubbletop P-47D.

Although it is still marketed today, this old kit lacks detailing, has a number of very noticeable inaccuracies, and it falls short of every other 1/48th scale Thunderbolt that is presently available. We cannot recommend any issue to the scale modeler.

The author used the original Hawk 1/48th scale kit to build this model of Major Robert S. Johnson's "Lucky." The kit has been reissued by Testors, and it remains available today over thirty years after its original release.

Lindberg P-47N Thunderbolt

Issued in the 1950s, this model had an electric motor, and it was the first 1/48th scale P-47N ever released. While the box art claims that the model is authentic, it is a claim that is not justified by what is inside the box. Although landing gear is provided, there are no wheel wells at all. There are inaccuracies throughout, and detailing is almost non-existent. This is a kit for collectors, not for modelers.

Monogram P-47D Razorback and Bubbletop Thunderbolts

When originally issued as a bubbletop P-47D, this kit was one of the first to help move scale modeling out of the realm of toys and into the art form of producing accurate and detailed replicas of the real thing. It featured a detailed cockpit tub, enclosed wheel wells with hydraulic lines and cylinders, and surface detailing that was more delicate and accurate than found on previous models. However, as did other kit manufacturers, Monogram mistakenly put an adjustable trim tab on both ailerons rather than on the left only. Interestingly, they made the mistake on the top of the right aileron but not the bottom.

Another error is that the guns are in line with the

Norris Graser used the Monogram 1/48th scale P-47D bubbletop to build this model of a Thunderbolt from 86th Fighter Squadron of the 79th Fighter Group. (Graser)

leading edge of the wing instead of being parallel to the ground. The engine is represented as a single piece that fits inside the cowling, and it has the duct work for the air scoop as well. While admittedly this is not the best solution, it looks quite good when completed.

Monogram used a well known but inaccurate set of drawings when developing this kit, and some inaccuracies appear on the fuselage of the bubbletop variant. But by the time the razorback version was released several years later, these had been noted and corrected. The effect of this can be seen if a fuselage half from the bubbletop kit is held next to the same half from the razorback issue. Most noticeably, the wing on the razorback release is about six scale inches further forward than on the bubbletop version. It is the razorback that is correct. Pending the release of the Hasegawa razorback kit, this Monogram release remains the most accurate P-47D razorback available in 1/48th scale. The sharp razorback spine is faithfully reproduced as is the slight bulging of the framed canopy. Revell-Monogram is reissuing this kit in early 1998, and it offers a reasonably priced alternative to the Hasegawa models.

The bubbletop releases come with a Hamilton-Standard propeller, a flat belly tank, and 500-pound bombs to go on the pylons under the wings. By comparison, the razorback version comes with the original Curtiss Electric thin-blade propeller, triple-tube rocket launchers, a 105-gallon paper tank, and two 500-pound bombs. For those who want additional tanks, KMC makes excellent ones that can be used on these or any other 1/48th scale Thunderbolts. KMC also has separate control surfaces that fit either of these Monogram models. Again, KMC makes all three paddleblade propellers that were used on P-47s, and these can be substituted when the modeler wants to use a different design than what is in the kit. To improve cockpit detail, the True Details cockpit set for the Hasegawa kits requires only a little filing and refitting in order to be used in either of these Monogram models.

In 1993, Monogram reissued the bubbletop version as a "high tech" kit with etched metal detailing parts. These included parts to enhance the cockpit, landing gear, pylons, and the bombs.

While the Hasegawa kits are newer and admittedly better than these from Monogram, these offer a more reasonably priced alternative. In particular, the razorback issue is very accurate and can easily be completed as an outstanding model.

Otaki/Arii P-47D Razorback Thunderbolt

This model ranks behind the Hasegawa, Monogram, and Academy kits when it comes to P-47Ds in 1/48th scale. Detailing in the cockpit and wheel wells is nowhere near as good or complete as found in the other three kits, and there are also some shape and outline problems. The cockpit floor is not corrugated as it should be, and the rudder pedals are too short due to the fact that the cockpit is too shallow.

The engine is about equal to that found in the Monogram kits. It is a single piece that includes the duct work for the air scoop. The propeller is a reasonable representation of the original Curtiss Electric type.

Two 500-pound bombs are provided for the wing pylons, and a 1000-pound bomb fits on the fuselage. There are no fuel tanks included, and these were almost always seen on Thunderbolts. The resin tanks available from KMC will help in solving this shortcoming.

Scribing is the recessed type, and it has several inaccuracies. As with most Thunderbolt kits, an adjustable trim tab is on both ailerons instead of just the left one. The balance tab is also missing from the right aileron.

In short, this model is not as good as the ones from Monogram, Academy, or Hasegawa. We recommend using one of those instead.

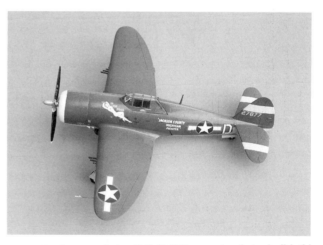

Stan Parker used the Arii P-47D razorback to build this model of "In The Mood." (Parker)

Revell-Monogram "ProModeler" Series P-47N Thunderbolt

When compared to the Academy/Minicraft P-47N in the same scale, this model is better in some respects, and worse in others. It has the correct propeller for a P-47N, that being the asymmetrical Curtiss Electric paddleblade type. It also has the correct engine with the cylindrical crankcase, and both rows of cylinders are molded as separate pieces. Most of the details in the cockpit are also better, but the instrument panel is noticeably too small. The instrument panel from the True Details cockpit set for the Academy/Minicraft model can be used to correct this deficiency if desired. However, it will take some trimming in order to get it to fit properly. Some modelers may find it simpler to use the entire True Details P-47N cockpit set and trim it to fit this model.

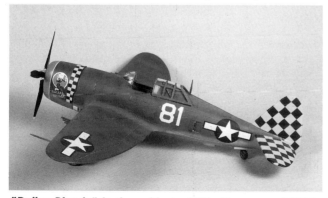

"Dallas Blonde" is the subject of this Monogram 1/48th scale P-47D razorback. It was built by Norris Graser, and it represents a P-47D-10-RE from the 319th Fighter Squadron of the 325th Fighter Group. (Graser)

Revell-Monogram added this 1/48th scale P-47N to its ProModeler line of kits in mid-1997. It was used by Jim Roeder to build this Thunderbolt from the 318th Fighter Group. (Roeder)

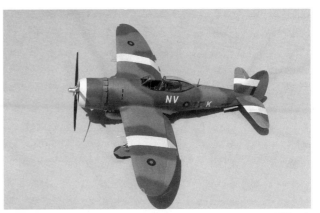

Revell has issued both razorback and bubbletop P-47Ds in 1/32nd scale. Frank Mitchell spent a lot of time correcting inaccuracies and improving detail to build this excellent model of a British Thunderbolt.

There is an error in the instructions. The right exhaust waste gate is part 3, and the left exhaust waste gate is part 4. The instructions have the part numbers reversed. The deflectors on these parts are represented more like doors covering vents instead of the deflectors for the oil cooler discharge air as they actually are.

The guns are aligned properly, and Revell-Monogram made an effort to do some extra detailing. In addition to the complete engine, the head of the turbosupercharger can be seen inside the shroud, and the main gear wheels have the correct number of spokes.

The model may be completed as a P-47N-1-RE without the rocket stubs under the wings. But the rockets are included, and the stubs are molded as part of the rocket bodies. Using the stub launchers without the rockets would necessitate removing them from the rockets first.

Access panels do not stand proud of the rest of the aircraft's skin as they do on the Academy/Minicraft kit, but the recessed panel lines are uneven in places. The forward cowl ring is noticeably smaller than the rest of the cowl, and this proves to be more difficult to correct than one might think. The skin is not polished smooth, and this could be a problem for a model with a natural metal finish. There are also some sink marks that need to be filled and sanded out.

The clear parts are well executed, but the windscreen mounts to a raised area on the fuselage. This is inaccurate in that no such area exists on the real aircraft.

In addition to the rockets, fuel tanks and bombs are provided as external stores. These are very accurate, and if not used on this kit, save them for use on other models.

Although not a bad kit, this model suffers from some faulty design and poor engineering. While it is better than the Academy/Minicraft in several areas, it is not quite as good overall. Perhaps the best way to proceed is to use parts from both kits to build a single model.

Jim Roeder contributed to this review.

1/32nd SCALE KIT

Revell P-47D Bubbletop and Razorback Thunderbolts
First released in 1969 as a P-47D bubbletop, this kit

and its razorback cousin remain the only Thunderbolt models available in 1/32nd scale. Most outlines are basically correct except for the vertical tail which must be completely reshaped along the leading edge.

The skin is covered with hundreds of rivets, and the only way to achieve acceptable results is to sand the entire model smooth and rescribe all panel lines by hand.

The propeller is the original Curtiss Electric design, but the blades need to be reshaped to match the drawings in this book. The engine has two complete rows of cylinders and a fairly accurate crankcase. But it provides only a starting point, and some detailing work will be necessary. The removable panels on each side of the cowling are bogus and should be glued in place.

The cockpit has some detailing, but it is neither complete nor accurate. Unfortunately, we know of no aftermarket detailing set for it, so everything must be done from scratch. The wheel wells are enclosed, but they need extra detailing. The guns should be removed from the wings and replaced with new ones which are aligned parallel to the ground instead of to the leading edge of the wings.

The pylons are only fair approximations of the real ones, and they have British style bombs on them. These should be removed and replaced with ones from another kit or an after-market source. The fuel tank that goes on the centerline station is also not very accurate and should be deleted or replaced.

The clear parts in both the bubbletop and razorback releases are thick and have distortions near the framework. It is best to make new ones using the heat-and-smash method of forming clear plastic. No clear parts are provided for any of the lights.

The landing gear struts and doors are usable, but the main gear wheels and tires need a lot of attention. The tires have no tread, and the wheel cover is not a flat disc as it should be.

If a modeler wants to take this kit down to the basics, correct some inaccuracies with respect to shape, add a lot of missing details, and rescribe all surface detail, a decent model can result. This is evidenced by Frank Mitchell's excellent Thunderbolt in British markings that is pictured with this review. But this takes a considerable amount of work and many hours to accomplish.